D1555036

DR. JIM DENISON

between
COMPROMISE
— and —
COURAGE

The Choice Every
Christian Must Make

ALSO BY DR. JIM DENISON

The Daily Article email newsletter is news discerned differently every Monday through Friday.
Subscribe for free at DenisonForum.org.

Biblical Insight to Tough Questions: Vols. 1–8

Every Hour I Need Thee: A Practical Guide to Daily Prayer

Blessed: Eight Ways Christians Change Culture

To Follow in His Footsteps: A Daily Devotional through the Holy Sites of Israel

Bright Hope for Tomorrow: How Jesus' Parables Illuminate Our Darkest Days

Respectfully, I Disagree: How to Be a Civil Person in an Uncivil Time

The Greater Work: How Prayer Positions You to Receive All that Grace Intends to Give

How Does God See America?

Request these books at DenisonForum.org/store

TABLE OF CONTENTS

FOREWORD

While discussing the controversy over removing statues, *CNN* commentator Don Lemon said that "Jesus Christ . . . was not perfect when he was here on this earth. So why are we deifying the founders of this country?" Lemon, who grew up Baptist and attended a Catholic school, was back in the news in 2021 for his attack on the Vatican's refusal to bless same-sex marriages. He stated that the Catholic Church and other churches should "reexamine themselves and their teachings because that is not what God is about. God is not about hindering people or even judging people."

Lemon's belief that he can dictate theology to the Catholic Church reflects the postmodern claim that personal beliefs are truth. If he says that God is "not about hindering people or even judging people," it must be so, at least in his mind. Lemon's belief that his beliefs reflect reality is akin to the man who once told me "I don't believe in hell" as though his belief changed the existence of hell. If I were to claim that "I don't believe in Canada," does that change the existence of Canada?

But there's a larger story behind this story, one that we urgently need to understand.

Don Lemon's "god" is the god of American culture today. Lemon also said, "I respect people's right to believe in whatever they want to believe in their God, but if you believe in something that hurts another person or does not give someone the same rights and freedoms—not necessarily under the Constitution because this is under God—I think that that's wrong." I am certain that a large number of Americans would agree. You are welcome to your beliefs in God unless someone disagrees. If anyone considers your beliefs to be hurtful to anyone, they must therefore be hurtful. And if they are hurtful, they must be disallowed.

This choice between compromise and courage is not new for God's people.

Think of the prophet Jeremiah, imprisoned in a cistern because he would not stop preaching God's word (Jeremiah 38:1–6). Remember Shadrach, Meshach, and Abednego in the fiery furnace (Daniel 3), Daniel in the lions' den (Daniel 6), Peter in Herod's prison (Acts 12), and John exiled on Patmos (Revelation 1).

The compromise we will be encouraged to make was just what the apostles were ordered to do by the supreme court of their day: "We strictly charged you not to teach in this name, yet here you have filled Jerusalem with your teaching" (Acts 5:28). If these believers would keep their beliefs to themselves and go along to get along, they would get along. However, the apostles replied: "We must obey God rather than men" (v. 29). When the council then "beat them and charged them not to speak in the name of Jesus" (v. 40), they left "rejoicing that they were counted worthy to suffer dishonor for the name" (v. 41).

Standing for biblical truth does not mean that we condemn others or consider ourselves to be better than them. It means that we love them enough to tell them the truth even—and especially—when they do not want to hear it. It means that we share with them the good news that has given us hope in the belief that it will do the same for them.

It's my hope and prayer that this book provides you with the truth of what the Bible says on seven of today's most pressing topics: racism, abortion, politics, religious liberty, removing statues, cancel culture, and suicide. You may note that issues pertaining to sexuality are not listed; because that topic is so expansive, we are writing a standalone book on what the Bible says about sexuality.

Please know that these chapters are adapted and updated from content previously published at DenisonForum. org. However, each chapter also includes discussion questions for personal or small group study. You may download the questions as a PDF at denisonforum.org/courage-questions or via the QR code.

When you next face the choice between compromise and courage, may these words and God's Spirit encourage you to boldness.

—Dr. Jim Denison

CHAPTER 1

THE GREATEST SIN IN AMERICA:
What does the Bible say about racism?

George Floyd, an unarmed African American, died in Minneapolis, Minnesota, on Memorial Day, May 25, 2020, after a White police officer knelt on his neck for almost nine minutes. Mr. Floyd was handcuffed and lying face down at the time. He repeatedly told the four police officers, "I can't breathe."

Two autopsies determined his death to be a homicide. The four police officers were fired the day after the tragedy. Derek Chauvin, the officer who knelt on Mr. Floyd's neck, was charged with second-degree murder and found guilty. The other three officers were charged with aiding and abetting second-degree murder. Demonstrations protesting against Mr. Floyd's death and racial injustice were staged in more than four hundred cities across America and around the world as well.

George Floyd's death followed the killing of Ahmaud Arbery, a twenty-five-year-old African American man who was jogging near his home on February 23, 2020. He was running in Satilla Shores, a community near Brunswick, Georgia, when he was confronted by two armed men in a pickup truck. Arbery was shot and killed. Charges of racism pervaded that tragedy from its inception. The two men who confronted Arbery were White. No arrests were made or charges filed until over two months after the shooting, when a video of the attack was made public. Many have asked if the same delay would have occurred if a White man had been the victim. The shooting highlights "a unique anxiety that has long troubled countless runners—running while black."

The deaths of George Floyd and Ahmaud Arbery add to the ever-growing list of names and places that have come to national attention due to racism. As such news happens with tragic regularity, what can a Christian do to fight racism?

To that end, let's look at racism's history in America, the role of slavery in the Bible, what the Bible says about racism, and our practical response as Christians to the problem of racism.

RACISM IN AMERICA

In 2019, Pew Research Center reported that "a majority of Americans say race relations in the United States are bad, and of those, about seven-in-ten say things are getting even worse." A generation after the 1954 Brown school desegregation decision, the Civil Rights Act of 1964, and the Voting Rights Act of 1965, racial discrimination continues in our country. According to the FBI, 60 percent of hate crimes are motivated by race, ethnicity, or ancestry.

RACISM AND INDIGENOUS AMERICANS

The Oxford English Dictionary defines racism as "prejudice, discrimination, or antagonism directed against someone of a different race based on the belief that one's own race is superior." By this definition, mistreating people of a particular race is "racism" to the degree that the perpetrator considers his or her victims to be racially inferior.

We find such attitudes on the part of Anglos toward non-Anglos since Europeans first landed in the New World. Many European explorers characterized the indigenous peoples they encountered as "heathen" and considered their race and culture to be inferior by nature. Many claimed that such people could be transformed by the introduction of Christianity and European customs. One colonist described native Americans as "having little of Humanitie but shape, ignorant of Civilitie, of Arts, of Religion; more brutish than the beasts they hunt, more wild and unmanly than the unmanned wild Countrey, which they range rather than inhabite; captivated also to Satans tyranny in foolish pieties, mad impieties, wicked idlenesse, busie and bloudy wickednesse."

RACISM AND AFRICANS

Many who supported the enslavement of Africans likewise viewed them as inferior to White people. An Anglican minister in Barbados claimed that "Negro's were Beasts, and had no more Souls than Beasts." Africans were considered intellectually and morally inferior to Whites; some declared that they were descended from apes. Such horrific claims were used to justify the system of chattel slavery (the personal ownership of a slave) that enslaved millions of Africans. Many slaveholders convinced themselves that slaves, due to their supposedly inferior nature, were better off and better cared for in bondage than in freedom.

This racist ideology led directly to America's "original sin," the institution of slavery in the New World. The first group of African slaves—four men and women—arrived at Jamestown, Virginia, in 1619. Planters quickly realized that enormous profits could be gained from importing enslaved laborers.

Africans could be made to work much longer and harder in the fields. Since they were so far from Africa, they could not easily escape and return home. In addition, African slaves came from a variety of nations and cultures and thus could not easily communicate with each other to organize resistance. Most slaves came from West Africa, where some tribal leaders were willing to capture and sell other Africans for profit. Slaves became especially important to the economy of the South, where the climate and topography were more suitable for tobacco and cotton plantations.

By 1860, the United States was divided into "slave" and "free" states. "There were four million slaves in the South, compared with less than 0.5 million free African Americans in all of the US. Of the 4.4 million African Americans in the US before the war, almost four million of these people were held as slaves; meaning that for all African Americans living in the US in 1860, there was an 89 percent chance that they lived in slavery."

While the Declaration of Independence claimed that "all men are created equal," the US Constitution determined that enslaved persons would be counted as "three-fifths of all other Persons" for purposes of government representation and taxation (Article I, Section II, Paragraph

III). The Constitution permitted importing slaves until 1808, with a tax of ten dollars per slave (Article I, Section IX, Clause I). And it required those living in free states to return escaped slaves to their owners (Article IV, Section II, Clause III).

Slavery was legal in America until 1865 and the adoption of the Thirteenth Amendment. The Fourteenth Amendment (1868) guaranteed the same rights to all male citizens; the Fifteenth Amendment (1870) made it illegal to deprive any eligible citizen of the right to vote, regardless of color. However, segregation in schools was not made illegal until *Brown v. Board of Education* in 1954. Jim Crow laws enforcing racial segregation were overturned by the Civil Rights Act of 1964 and the Voting Rights Act of 1965.

RACISM AND ASIANS

Asian immigrants have faced racial prejudice in the US as well. Those who came to America to work in mines, farms, and railroads were willing to accept lower wages, which enraged White residents. As a result, Asians became the victims of riots and attacks. The 1882 Chinese Exclusion Act and the 1924 Asian Exclusion Act barred additional immigration. These acts also declared Asians ineligible for citizenship, which meant they could not own land.

More recently, racism against Asian Americans rose in 2020. According to Russell Jeung, chair of Asian American studies at San Francisco State University, there was "a 50-percent rise in coverage of anti-Asian racism linked to the new coronavirus between early February and early March," and he predicted that "many more take place that never make the news."

In other words, racism is not only a historical fact; it's a present-day reality.

RACISM TODAY

Studies show that racism persists in America:

1. People with "black-sounding names" had to send out 50 percent more job applications than people with "white-sounding names" to get a callback.

2. A Black man is three times more likely to be searched at a traffic stop and six times more likely to go to jail than a White man.

3. If a Black person kills a White person, he or she is twice as likely to receive the death sentence as a White person who kills a Black person.

4. Black people serve up to 20 percent more time in prison than White people for the same crimes.

5. Black people are 38 percent more likely to be sentenced to death than White people for the same crimes.

Racism persists in America's churches as well:

1. Only 32 percent of White pastors strongly agree that "my church is involved with racial reconciliation at the local level." Fifty-three percent of African American pastors strongly agree with this statement.

2. Only 56 percent of evangelicals believe that "people of color are often put at a social disadvantage because of their race." Eighty-four percent of Blacks agree with this statement.

3. A 2015 study showed that 81 percent of America's Protestant churches were composed of one predominant racial group.

4. While 90 percent of Protestant pastors say their congregation would welcome a sermon on racial reconciliation, only 26 percent say leaders in their church have encouraged them to preach on the subject.

Dr. Martin Luther King Jr. was right: Sunday morning worship services are still the most segregated hour in America.

SLAVERY IN THE BIBLE

When my family moved to Atlanta in 1994, we quickly fell in love with the Old South. Being from Texas, I thought something was historical if it happened while Tom Landry was coach of the Cowboys. Southern history goes back to the Revolutionary War and colonial times. I was especially fascinated by the Civil War (though Southerners will say that "there was nothing civil about it").

But there's a dark side to the story. While traveling one day in the beautiful city of Charleston, South Carolina, my wife and I came upon a "slave-trading warehouse." This was the horrific place where slaves were brought to America on ships and then sold at market in chains. I can still remember the crumbling limestone building and my revulsion upon seeing it. I believe that racism is the greatest sin in America, the failure which keeps us from addressing our other failures. Racism makes crime in south Dallas a "Black" problem and drug abuse in north Dallas a "White" problem when they're both our problems. Given our tragic history with racism, thinking about the subject of slavery in the Bible is a bit repugnant for most of us. However, since many say the Bible was wrong on this issue, we must discuss this painful subject briefly.

SLAVERY IN THE OLD TESTAMENT

It is an unfortunate fact that slavery was an accepted part of life in the ancient world. No early society or literature questioned its existence or necessity.

People in Old Testament times became slaves in a variety of ways:

- They were born to enslaved parents (Genesis 17:23).

- They were purchased as slaves (Genesis 37:28)

- They sold themselves to pay a debt (Leviticus 25:39–55).

- Breaking into a home was punished by enslavement (Exodus 22:3).

- Prisoners of war were commonly enslaved (Joel 3:6).

- And the children of Israel enslaved the Canaanites they conquered in the Promised Land (Judges 1:28).

Slaves in Israel were considered property to be bought and sold (Exodus 21:32). However, they were granted protection against murder, permanent injury, or undue physical labor (Exodus 21:20, 26; 23:12). Hebrew household slaves were included at religious meals (Exodus 12:44). Such privileges and protections were extremely rare in the ancient world. But why did the Old Testament not condemn this practice?

In many ways, it did. There were several ways a Hebrew slave could be freed (a process called "manumission"):

- An individual could be purchased and set free (Exodus 21:8).

- A slave permanently injured by his master was to be set free (Exodus 21:26).

- Hebrews were to be held as slaves for no longer than six years (Deuteronomy 15:12).

- The Jubilee Year, which occurred every forty-nine years, was to free all Israelite slaves (Leviticus 25:50).

- But still we ask: Why did the Old Testament sanction this practice at all? Its rules minimized this evil, protected slaves from physical harm, and provided for their eventual freedom. But the New Testament gives us God's complete word on the subject.

SLAVERY IN THE NEW TESTAMENT

In the Old Testament era, people were enslaved primarily through war. But in the first century AD, the procreation of slaves swelled their numbers enormously. And many people actually sold themselves into slavery to improve their lives. Owning and using people as slaves was so common in the Roman Empire that not a single Roman writer condemned the practice. But this acceptance of slavery would begin to change with the growth and influence of Christianity.

Slavery in the Roman era was dramatically different from the despicable practice in American history. If you walked through any first-century Roman city, you would not be able to tell most slaves from free people. Slaves performed manual labor, but they were also doctors, nurses, household managers, and intellectuals. They managed finances and cities. They were often given an excellent education at the expense of their owners, with the result that philosophers and tutors were typically slaves.

Even more amazing to us, it was common for people to sell themselves into slavery to secure such privileges. A person who wanted to be a Roman citizen could sell himself to a citizen and then purchase his freedom. For many people, slavery was more a process than a condition.

While there is no doubt that many slaves were abused physically, sexually, and socially, many were part of the more privileged strata of society. The total dependence of the Roman economy upon the labor of slaves made it impossible for the ancient world to conceive of abolishing this institution. If an economist were to propose that we refuse all goods and services imported from outside America, we'd be equally surprised. As a result, no New Testament writer attempted to end slavery itself, as this was not possible in their time. But several other facts should be noted as well.

One: Paul abolished all racial and social discrimination for Christians.

"In Christ Jesus you are all sons of God, through faith. For as many of you as were baptized into Christ have put on Christ. There is neither Jew nor Greek, there is neither slave nor free, there is no male and female, for you are all one in Christ Jesus" (Galatians 3:26–28). Every believer is our sister or brother. None in the Christian family are to be viewed as slaves.

Two: Free Christians viewed slaves as their equal.

Paul appealed to Philemon to see his slave, Onesimus, "no longer as a bondservant but more than a bondservant, as a beloved brother" (Philemon 16). Clement, a friend of Paul, wrote in his letter to the Corinthians (ca. AD 90), "We know many among ourselves who have given themselves up to bonds, in order that they might ransom others. Many, too, have surrendered themselves to slavery, that with the price which they received for themselves, they might provide food for others." Ignatius (died AD 107) wrote to Polycarp: "Do not despise either male or female slaves, yet neither let them be puffed up with conceit, but rather let them submit themselves the more, for the glory of God, that they may obtain from God a better liberty."

Three: The New Testament church gave those who were enslaved a family and a home.

This was one reason why so many of the earliest believers were slaves. Pastors and church leaders came from the ranks both of slaves and free. Christians made no distinction between the two, for their Father welcomed all as his children.

Four: Not a single New Testament leader owned slaves, even though many had the resources to purchase them.

Their example inspired William Wilberforce and countless other Christians to do all they could to abolish slavery, and we thank God that they were successful.

RACISM AND THE BIBLE

The Bible clearly condemns all forms of racism and views every person as equally valuable. Let's look at what God's word says about our subject, then we'll consider some common questions people ask about the Scriptures and racism.

SIX THEOLOGICAL FACTS

One: We are all created by God.

The human story begins in Genesis 1, where God "created man in his own image, in the image of God he created him; male and female he created them" (v. 27). Every person is created intentionally by God in his own divine image. Thus, every person is sacred and equally valuable. Every form of racism, by definition, is to be rejected.

Two: We are all descended from the same parents.

Every human being is descended from Adam and Eve (Genesis 1:28). As a result, "The man called his wife's name Eve, because she was the mother of all living" (Genesis 3:20). As Scripture notes, the Lord "made from one man every nation of mankind to live on all the face of the earth" (Acts 17:26). Because of the Flood, all of humanity can trace our ancestry to Noah as well (Genesis 9:1).

Three: Every person is equally valuable to God.

As noted earlier, Paul stated boldly: "There is neither Jew nor Greek, there is neither slave nor free, there is no male and female, for you are all one in Christ Jesus" (Galatians 3:28). This was written at a time when many Jews considered Greeks to be unclean and inferior. Some claimed that God made Gentiles so there would be "firewood in hell." Many refused even to look upon a Gentile in public.

For their part, Gentiles persecuted the Jewish people across nearly their entire history. The Jews were enslaved by Egypt, attacked by Canaanites and other surrounding tribes, destroyed by Assyria, enslaved by Babylon, and ruled by Persia, Greece, and Rome. The Roman Empire destroyed their temple in AD 70 and disbanded their nation after the Bar Kochba revolt in AD 132–135. Nonetheless, Scripture teaches that "there is neither Jew nor Greek" in the eyes of God.

"There is neither slave nor free" was also a revolutionary claim. As we have seen, slavery was endemic in the first-century world. Many viewed slaves, especially those who came from foreign lands, as inferior to Romans. "There is no male and female" was a radical statement as well. Romans considered women to be the possession of men. A female belonged to her father until she belonged to her husband. Women were either wives or concubines, with few rights of their own.

Galatians 3:28 sounds the clarion call that every form of racism known to Paul's day was invalid and sinful. The God who made us all loves us all. Paul repeated his assertion to the Colossians: "There is not Greek and Jew, circumcised and uncircumcised, barbarian, Scythian, slave, free; but Christ is all, and in all" (Colossians 3:11). To summarize: "God shows no partiality" (Acts 10:34).

Four: Each person is equally welcome to salvation in Christ.

God loves all sinners and wants all to come to faith in his Son: "God shows his love for us in that while we were still sinners, Christ died for us" (Romans 5:8). Our Lord "is patient toward you, not wishing that any should perish, but that all should reach repentance" (2 Peter 3:9). As Paul noted, God "desires all people to be saved and to come to the knowledge of the truth" (1 Timothy 2:4). That's why the apostle could testify: "I am not ashamed of the gospel, for it is the power of God for salvation to everyone who believes, to the Jew first and also to the Greek" (Romans 1:16).

Our Father's saving love is available to all: "There is no distinction between Jew and Greek; for the same Lord is Lord of all, bestowing his riches on all who call on him" (Romans 10:12). His grace is universal: "For God so loved the world, that he gave his only Son, that whoever believes in him should not perish but have eternal life" (John 3:16).

When we trust in Christ, we become one people: "He himself is our peace, who has made us both one and has broken down in his flesh the dividing wall of hostility" (Ephesians 2:14). As a result, "In one Spirit we were all baptized into one body—Jews or Greeks, slaves or free— and all were made to drink of one Spirit" (1 Corinthians 12:13).

Jesus "is the propitiation for our sins, and not for ours only but also for the sins of the whole world" (1 John 2:2). Peter told his fellow Jewish Christians that God "made no distinction between [Gentile Christians] and us, having cleansed their hearts by faith" (Acts 15:9). As a result, we are to "make disciples of all nations" (Matthew 28:19). "Nations" translates *ethnos*, meaning people groups. We get "ethnicity" from this word. Every person of every ethnicity is to be brought to Christ through the ministry of the church.

Five: All people will be equally valuable in paradise.

John was given this vision of heaven: "After this I looked, and behold, a great multitude that no one could number, from every nation, from all tribes and peoples and languages, standing before the throne and before the Lamb, clothed in white robes, with palm branches in their hands" (Revelation 7:9).

Six: We are to love all people unconditionally.

God's word is blunt: "If you show partiality, you are committing sin and are convicted by the law as transgressors" (James 2:9). "Partiality" translates *prosopolempsia*, meaning to show favoritism or prejudice, to treat one person as inherently better than another. Such prejudice is "sin."

God told his people: "You shall treat the stranger who sojourns with you as the native among you, and you shall love him as yourself, for you were strangers in the land of Egypt" (Leviticus 19:34). Jesus taught us: "Whatever you wish that others would do to you, do also to them, for this is the Law and the Prophets" (Matthew 7:12). We are to "love your neighbor as yourself" (Matthew 22:39, quoting Leviticus 19:18).

Peter testified to the Gentiles who sought to hear the gospel: "You yourselves know how unlawful it is for a Jew to associate with or to visit anyone of another nation, but God has shown me that I should not call any person common or unclean" (Acts 10:28).

THREE COMMON QUESTIONS

One: What about the "mark of Cain"?

After Cain murdered his brother, God sentenced him to be "a fugitive and a wanderer on the earth" (Genesis 4:12). Cain protested that "I shall be a fugitive and a wanderer on the earth, and whoever finds me will kill me" (v. 14). God replied, "Not so! If anyone kills Cain, vengeance shall be taken on him sevenfold" (v. 15a). Then, "the LORD put a mark on Cain, lest any who found him should attack him" (v. 15b). The Hebrew word translated "mark" is *ot*, referring to a sign or token. It is used eighty times in the Old Testament; not once does it refer to skin color.

Nonetheless, some have identified this "mark" with being Black. Since Cain was cursed for his sin against his brother, it was claimed that those whose skin was black were his descendants and were cursed by God. This claim was used to justify the enslavement of Africans. This line of reasoning is completely wrong. As noted, the "mark" of Cain had nothing to do with his skin color. In addition, Cain's family line probably died in the Flood.

And note that Moses married a "Cushite woman" (Numbers 12:1). Cush was a region south of Ethiopia; its people were known for their black skin (Jeremiah 13:23). When Moses' brother and sister spoke against him for marrying his Cushite wife, God rebuked them (Numbers 12:4–15). Clearly, the "mark of Cain" has nothing to do with Black people.

Two: What about the "curse of Ham"?

Ham was one of Noah's three sons. Ham had four sons: Cush, Egypt, Put, and Canaan (Genesis 10:6). Ham is considered the father of Black people since some of his descendants settled in Africa. According to tradition, Cush settled in Ethiopia, south of Egypt; Egypt (also known as "Mizraim") settled in the land of Egypt; Put settled in Libya; Canaan settled above Africa and east of the Mediterranean Sea.

The Bible tells us that after the Flood, Noah became drunk (Genesis 9:21). Then "Ham, the father of Canaan, saw the nakedness of his father and told his two brothers outside" (v. 22). Shem and Japheth "covered the nakedness of their father" (v. 23). After Noah awoke, he said, "Cursed be Canaan; a servant of servants shall he be to his brothers" (v. 25). Note that Noah cursed Canaan, not Ham. Thus, his curse was irrelevant to Ham's sons who had settled in Africa and their descendants. Also note that Noah's curse was specifically directed at Canaan, with no mention of his descendants. If Noah's curse was applied to his descendants, it related to the Canaanites living in the land that became Israel. It had nothing whatever to do with Black people.

Nonetheless, the Old Scofield Reference Bible of 1909 (often considered the authoritative Bible of fundamentalist Christians) interprets Genesis 9:24–25 to teach: "A prophetic declaration is made that from Ham will descend an inferior and servile posterity." With his typically brilliant exposition, Dr. Tony Evans addresses this issue, noting that biblical curses are limited to three or four generations (Exodus 20:5) and are reversed when people repent and return to obedience (Exodus 20:6). As Dr. Evans shows, Scripture consistently rebukes and rejects the claim that Black people (or any other race) are inferior to any other.

Three: Didn't slavery proponents use the Bible to justify their position?

Tragically, many who supported slavery in the antebellum South used the "mark of Cain" and "curse of Ham" to justify their position. They also noted biblical statements encouraging slaves to obey their masters.

As we saw in the section on slavery, the Bible deals realistically with the practice where necessary, but it clearly endorses the intrinsic sacred value of each person. The biblical emphasis on the sanctity of life was one of the key motivating factors for William Wilberforce and others who worked so sacrificially to abolish slavery.

Like any other book, the Bible can be misused by those who misinterpret and misrepresent its teachings. For instance, when chloroform was developed, some were resistant to using it for women in childbirth since Genesis 3:16 teaches "in pain you shall bring forth children." When oil wells were first dug in Pennsylvania, many New York ministers opposed the project on the grounds that it would deplete the oil stored for the predestined burning of the world (2 Peter 3:10, 12). And winnowing fans were rejected by Christians who thought they interfered with the providence of God since "the wind blows where it wishes" (John 3:8). (For these and other examples, see John P. Newport and William Cannon's book, *Why Christians Fight Over the Bible*.)

When a doctor misuses medicine, we blame the physician, not the science. When an attorney misrepresents a legal statute, we blame the lawyer, not the law. In responding to racists who misused the Bible to justify slavery, we should blame the racists, not the word of God.

PRACTICAL RESPONSES

God's word clearly calls us to love every person as unconditionally as he loves us. How do we put such love into practice today?

One: Search your own heart.

A 2018 survey reported that 64 percent of Americans considered racism a major problem in our society and politics. Only 3 percent said it once existed but no longer does; only 1 percent said it had never been a major problem. Why is racism so pervasive and perennial in our culture?

In *Mere Christianity*, C. S. Lewis wrote: "If anyone would like to acquire humility, I can, I think, tell him the first step. The first step is to realize that one is proud. And a biggish step, too. At least, nothing whatever can be done before it. If you think you are not conceited, it means you are very conceited indeed." I think his logic applies to the issue of racism as well.

One reason racial discrimination is such a perennial problem is that it appeals to the core of our sin nature. In the Garden of Eden, the serpent promised the woman that if she ate of the forbidden fruit, "you will be like God" (Genesis 3:5). From then to now, our desire to be our own god is at the root of all our sin. As Friedrich Nietzsche noted, the "will to power" is the basic drive in human nature.

Here's my point: Racism is a way to feel superior to others on the basis of immutable realities. If I'm White and you're Black, I will always be White and you will always be Black. If I delude myself into believing that being White is superior to being Black, I will therefore always feel superior to you. This temptation is alluring on levels we often don't recognize. In fact, I think Satan wants us not to acknowledge our discriminatory inclinations lest we admit and repent of them.

It is therefore a good first step in confronting racism to check ourselves. Ask the Holy Spirit to show you any unstated attitudes or assumptions that are discriminatory. Ask him to reveal to you any thoughts, words, or actions that are racist. Pray regularly for such discernment. And where necessary, repent.

Two: Take the cultural initiative.

"In some ways, it's super simple. People learn to be whatever their society and culture teaches them. We often assume it takes parents actively teaching their kids, for them to be racist. The truth is that unless parents actively teach kids not to be racists, they will be." This is how Jennifer Richeson, a Yale University social psychologist, explains the continued pervasiveness of racism. She continues: "This is not the product of some deep-seated, evil heart that is cultivated. It comes from the environment, the air all around us."

Eric Knowles, a psychology professor at New York University, adds: "There's a lot of evidence that people have an ingrained even evolved tendency toward people who are in our so-called 'in group.'" What is the solution?

"The only way to change bias is to change culture," according to Richeson. "You have to change what is acceptable in society. People today complain about politically correct culture, but what that does is provide a check on people's outward attitude, which in turn influences how we think about ourselves internally. Everything we're exposed to gives us messages about who is good and bad." Such change starts with us. Christians are "the salt of the earth" and "the light of the world" (Matthew 5:13, 14). If food lacks salt, the fault is not with the food. If a dark room lacks light, the fault is not with the room.

You and I must set the standard in our churches, communities, and families. We must be the change we want to see. We must take proactive, positive, initiatory steps to model the inclusive love of Jesus.

Three: Be the church.

On July 12, 2016, President George W. Bush spoke at a memorial service held in Dallas for police officers who had been killed in the line of duty. He made this remarkable point: "Americans, I think, have a great advantage. To renew our unity, we only need to remember our values. We have never been held together by blood or background. We are bound by things of the spirit, by shared commitments to common ideals."

President Bush is right. Many nations find their unity in a monolithic racial heritage, culture, or history. But America has never been about such uniformity. From the beginning, we were home to Protestants and Catholics and Jews, immigrants from across Europe and around the world. As a result, our truest unity will never be horizontal, only vertical. President Bush continued: "At our best, we honor the image of God we see in one another. We recognize that we are brothers and sisters, sharing the same brief moment on Earth and owing each other the loyalty of our shared humanity." In other words, the closer we draw to our Father, the closer we draw to each other.

That's why the gospel of God's reconciling love is the only transforming answer to the challenges we face. Legislation and the civil rights movement were essential to improving the lives of those who faced legalized discrimination. But laws cannot change people. Only the Spirit can do that. As a result, Christians are on the front lines of this spiritual battle for the soul and future of our nation.

Writing for the *Washington Post*, Dr. Evans traced our racial challenges "directly to ineffective Christians" and stated, "One of the real tragedies today is that the Church as a whole has not furthered God's light, equity, love and principles in our land in order to be a positive influence and impact for good in the midst of darkness, fear and hate."

He called for churches to unite in a "solemn assembly" with prayer and fasting, to train our members to be verbal and visible followers of Jesus, and to unite for good works in our communities. This is our "God-given role of influencing the conscience of our culture." Without it "our country will keep spiraling downward into the depths of fear and hate."

The time has come for the church to be the church.

CONCLUSION

Every person of every race was created by the same God in his image. Every one.

Early Christians believed this transforming truth. In the second century, Justin Martyr said of his fellow Christians: "We who hated and destroyed one another, and on account of their different manners would not live with men of a different tribe, now, since the coming of Christ, live familiarly with them, and pray for our enemies."

Clement of Alexandria described the true Christian: "Through the perfection of his love he impoverishes himself that he may never overlook a brother in affliction, especially if he knows that he could himself bear want better than his brother."

An early Christian named Minucius Felix told the Romans, "We love one another . . . with a mutual love, because we do not know how to hate." Tertullian, a second-century theologian, reported that pagans said of Christians, "See how they love one another."

Now it's our turn.

A DISCUSSION GUIDE ON RACISM

The following discussion guide may be used in a small group setting or for your personal time of devotion. We hope it helps you both better understand the topic and how God might want to use you, in your specific context, to be "salt and light" on this issue. A PDF download is available at denisonforum.org/courage-questions.

1. What is the most recent race-related death you've read or seen in the news?

2. How did your family or friends respond to that news?

3. How did you respond?

4. Why is it important to know the history of racism in America?

5. Considering racism in the church, how can your church increase its diversity?

6. Recall Martin Luther King Jr.'s famous quote that Sunday morning worship services are the most segregated hour in America. When that is the case, is it necessarily the result of racism? Can you think of any alternative reasons why Sunday morning worship services might be predominantly one race? What are some ways churches that are not multiracial can partner with other Christians to model the diversity of God's kingdom?

7. "Racism makes crime in south Dallas a 'Black' problem and drug abuse in north Dallas a 'White' problem when they're both our problems." What's the problem with designating social issues to certain races?

8. Before reading this chapter, what did you know about slavery in the Bible?

9. The conceptions and reality of slavery in the Bible are different from those of slavery in America's history. Recall the following important biblical events/statements against slavery in the New Testament:

   • Paul abolished all racial and social discrimination for Christians.

   • Free Christians viewed slaves as their equal.

   • The New Testament church gave those who were enslaved a family and a home.

   • Not a single New Testament leader owned slaves, even though many had the resources to purchase them.

   Which points stand out to you? Why? Note the biblical references in this chapter. What do these biblical truths tell you about the early church? How do their practices inform our ideas of church today?

10. Do any of the six theological facts in the subsection "Racism and the Bible" stand out to you as particularly significant? If so, why?

11. Why is it important that we base our beliefs about community on these theological facts?

12. Were you aware of the arguments of the mark of Cain and the curse of Ham before reading this chapter? Do you agree or disagree with the stance taken in this chapter? Why?

13. "In responding to racists who misused the Bible to justify slavery, we should blame the racists, not the word of God." Why is this an important distinction?

14. Why is searching our hearts such a necessary and "good first step"?

15. In your local community, how can you actively seek to change culture?

16. Why is it important that we continually return to God and his truth when we think about aspects of community?

17. How can you make loving others more of a priority in your life?

CHAPTER 2

THE MORAL ISSUE OF OUR TIME:
What does the Bible say about abortion?

Every year, more than thirty-six thousand people die on US highways.

Every twenty-one days, that many abortions are performed in America.

Since the Supreme Court's *Roe v. Wade* decision legalized abortion in 1973, more than sixty-one million abortions have been performed in America.

This number is larger than the combined populations of Alabama, Louisiana, Kentucky, Oregon, Oklahoma, Connecticut, Utah, Iowa, Nevada, Arkansas, Mississippi, Kansas, New Mexico, Nebraska, West Virginia, Idaho, Hawaii, New Hampshire, Maine, Montana, Rhode Island, Delaware, South Dakota, North Dakota, Alaska, Vermont, Wyoming, and Washington DC.

Or, put more simply, more abortions have been performed since 1973 than the population of over half the states in the US. And while those numbers have been declining year-to-year recently, almost 620,000 abortions were performed in 2018, the most recent year for which such data is available.

Abortion is *the* moral issue of our time.

It seems impossible to wrestle with the difficult issues of our day without addressing this crucial debate. Most conservative Christians believe that life begins at conception and abortion is therefore wrong. But are we sure? Is this a biblical fact?

If the answer is clear, why have so many denominational leaders taken pro-choice positions?

Is there a biblical, cohesive, practical position on this difficult subject?

I began this essay with the conviction that the pro-life position is most biblical. But I did not know much about the legal issues involved, or the theological arguments for a woman's right to choose abortion.

As you will see, the debate is much more complex than either side's rhetoric might indicate. But I believe that there is an ethical position which even our relativistic society might embrace.

PRO-LIFE VS. PRO-CHOICE

An "abortion" occurs when a "conceptus" is caused to die. To clarify vocabulary, "conceptus" is a general term for pre-born life growing in the mother's womb.

More specifically, doctors often speak of the union of a sperm and an ovum as a "zygote." A growing zygote is an "embryo." When the embryo reaches around seven weeks of age, it is called a "fetus." However, "fetus" is usually used in the abortion debate to describe all pre-born life.

- A "miscarriage" is a spontaneous, natural abortion.

- An "indirect abortion" occurs when actions taken to cure the mother's illness cause the unintended death of the fetus.

- A "direct abortion" occurs when action is taken to cause the intended death of the fetus.

- Why do so many people in America believe that a mother should have the right to choose direct abortion?

In 1973, the Supreme Court issued *Roe v. Wade,* its landmark abortion ruling. In essence, the Court overturned state laws limiting a woman's right to abortion. Its decision was largely based on the argument that the Constitution nowhere defines a fetus as a person or protects the rights of the unborn.

Rather, the Court determined that an unborn baby possesses only "potential life" and is not yet a "human being" or "person." It argued that every constitutional reference to "person" relates to those already born. The Fourteenth Amendment guarantees protections and rights to individuals, but the Court ruled that the amendment does not include the unborn.

The Court further determined that a woman's "right to privacy" extends to her ability to make her own choices regarding her health and body. Just as she has the right to choose to become pregnant, she has the right to end that pregnancy.

The Court suggested several specific reasons why she might choose abortion:

- "specific and direct harm" may come to her

- "maternity, or additional offspring, may force upon the woman a distressful life and future"

- "psychological harm may be imminent"

- "mental and physical health may be taxed by child care"

- problems may occur associated with bearing unwanted children

- and "the additional difficulties and continuing stigma of unwed motherhood" should be considered.

Since 1973, four positions have been taken in the abortion debate:

- There should be no right to an abortion, even to save the life of the mother. This has been the Catholic Church's usual position.

- Therapeutic abortions can be performed to save the mother's life.

- Extreme case abortions can be permitted in cases of rape, incest, or severe deformation of the fetus. Most pro-life advocates would accept therapeutic and extreme case abortions.

- Abortion should be available to any woman who chooses it. This is the typical "pro-choice" position.

MORAL ARGUMENTS FOR ABORTION

"Pro-choice" advocates make five basic claims:

1. No one can say when a fetus becomes a person, so the mother is the most appropriate person to make decisions regarding it.

2. Abortion must be protected so a woman who is the victim of rape or incest does not have to bear a child resulting from such an attack.

3. No unwanted child should be brought into the world.

4. The state has no right to legislate personal morality.

5. A woman must be permitted to make pregnancy decisions in light of her life circumstances.

Many theologians, pastors, and denominational leaders consider these claims to be both biblical and moral.

First, "pro-choice" proponents argue that a fetus is not legally a "person."

They agree with the Supreme Court's finding that the Constitution nowhere grants legal standing to a pre-born life. Only 40 to 50 percent of fetuses survive to become persons in the full sense. A fetus belongs to the mother until it attains personhood and is morally subject to any action she wishes to take with it.

Second, abortion must be protected as an alternative for women who are victims of rape or incest.

While this number is admittedly small in this country (approximately one percent of all abortions), it is growing in many countries around the world. As many as one in three women may become the victim of such an attack. They must be spared the further trauma of pregnancy and childbirth.

Third, no unwanted children should be brought into the world.

If a woman does not wish to bear a child, she clearly will not be an appropriate or effective mother if the child is born. Given the population explosion occurring in many countries of the world, abortion is a necessary option for women who do not want children. The woman is more closely involved with the fetus than any other individual and is the best person to determine whether or not this child is wanted and will receive proper care.

Fourth, the state has no right to legislate our personal moral decisions.

The government has no authority to restrict homosexuality, consensual sex, cigarette consumption, or other individual decisions that many people consider to be wrong. Since there is no constitutional standard for when life begins, decisions made regarding a fetus are likewise a matter for individual morality.

The state should impose legislation on moral questions only when this legislation expresses the clear moral consensus of the community and when it prevents conduct which obviously threatens the public welfare. Nearly everyone condemns murder, for instance, and believes that it threatens us all. But Americans are divided on the morality of abortion. It is hard to see how aborting a fetus threatens the rest of the community.

And so abortion should not be subject to governmental control. It is better to allow a mother to make this decision than to legislate it through governmental action. Many who personally consider abortion to be wrong are persuaded by this argument and thus support the "pro-choice" position.

Fifth, the rights and concerns of the mother must take precedence over those of the fetus.

Even if we grant fetuses limited rights, they must not supersede the rights of mothers, as the latter are clearly persons under the Constitution. If we allow abortion to protect her physical life, we should do so to protect her emotional health or quality of life as well.

This was one of the Court's most significant arguments, as it sought to protect the mother's mental and physical health. Many "pro-choice" advocates are especially persuaded by this argument and view the abortion debate within the context of a woman's right to control her own life.

MORAL ARGUMENTS AGAINST ABORTION

"Pro-life" advocates counter each of these claims with their own ethical arguments.

First, they assert that a fetus is a human life and should be granted the full protection of the law.

The fetus carries its parents' genetic code and is a distinct person. It does not yet possess self-consciousness, reasoning ability, or moral awareness (the usual descriptions of a "person"), but neither do newborns or young children. As this is the central issue of the debate, we'll say more about it in a moment.

Second, most "pro-life" advocates are willing to permit abortion in cases of rape or incest or to protect the life of the mother.

Since such cases typically account for only one to four percent of abortions performed, limiting abortion to these conditions would prevent the vast majority of abortions occurring in America.

Third, "pro-life" advocates agree that all children should be wanted, so they argue strongly for adoption as an alternative to abortion.

They also assert that an unwanted child would rather live than die. By "pro-choice" logic, it would be possible to argue for infanticide and all forms of euthanasia as well as abortion.

Fourth, "pro-life" supporters do not see abortion legislation as an intrusion into areas of private morality.

Protecting the rights of the individual is the state's first responsibility. No moral state can overlook murder, whatever the personal opinions of those who commit it. The state is especially obligated to protect the rights of those who cannot defend themselves.

But what of the claim that legislation must always reflect the clear will of the majority and protect the public welfare?

The collective will of the culture must never supersede what is right and wrong. For instance, marijuana is so popular that as many as 100 million Americans say they've tried it at least once. Nonetheless, we ban it because its harmful effects are clear to medical science. The effects of abortion on a fetus are obviously much more disastrous to the fetus.

And just because society is unclear as to when life begins does not mean that the question is unknowable.

If more of the public understood the physical and ethical issues involved in abortion, the large majority would consider abortion to be a threat to public welfare. Abortion threatens the entire community in three ways:

1. Abortion ends the lives of millions, on a level exceeding all wars and disasters combined.

2. Abortion encourages sexual promiscuity.

3. Abortion permits women to make a choice that will plague many of them with guilt for years to come.

And so abortion meets the standard for legislative relevance and must be addressed and limited or abolished by the state.

Fifth, "pro-life" advocates want to encourage the health of both the mother and the child and do not believe that we must choose between the two.

As the rights of a mother are no more important than those of her newborn infant, so they are no more important than those of her pre-born child. The stress, guilt, and long-term mental anguish reported by many who abort their children must be considered. The legal right to abortion subjects a woman to pressure from her husband or sexual partner to end her pregnancy. Killing the fetus for the sake of the mother's health is like remedying paranoia by killing all the imagined persecutors. For these reasons, "pro-life" advocates argue that a moral state must limit or prevent abortion. (For more on the ethical arguments for and against abortion see Milton A. Gonsalves' *Right & Reason: Ethics in Theory and Practice, 9th ed.*)

WHEN DOES LIFE BEGIN?

This is obviously the crucial question in the abortion debate. If life does not begin until the fetus is viable or the child is born, one can argue that the "right to life" does not extend to the pre-born and abortion should be considered both legal and moral. But if life begins at conception, there can be no moral justification for abortion, since this action kills an innocent person.

There are essentially three answers to our question:

- **"Functionalism"** states that the fetus is a "person" when it can act personally as a moral, intellectual, and spiritual agent. (Note that by this definition, some question whether a newborn infant would be considered a "person.")

- **"Actualism"** is the position that a fetus is a person if it possesses the potential for developing self-conscious, personal life. This definition would permit abortion when the fetus clearly does not possess the capacity for functional life.

- **"Essentialism"** argues that the fetus is a person from conception, whatever its health or potential. It is an individual in the earliest stages of development and deserves all the protections afforded to other persons by our society.

Our Declaration of Independence begins, "We hold these truths to be self-evident: that all men are created equal; that they are endowed by their creator with certain inalienable rights; that among these are life, liberty, and the pursuit of happiness." If an unborn child is considered a person, it possesses the "inalienable" right to life as well.

So, can we determine when life begins?

Our answer depends on the definition of *life*. A "pro-choice" advocate recognizes that the fetus is alive in the sense that it is a biological entity. But so is every other part of a woman's body. Some consider the fetus to be a "growth" and liken it to a tumor or other unwanted tissue. Biology alone is not enough to settle the issue.

What about capacity?

Many ethicists define a "person" as someone able to respond to stimuli, interact with others, and make individual decisions. A fetus meets the first two standards from almost the moment of its conception and clearly cannot fulfill the third only because it is enclosed in its mother's body. Would a newborn baby fulfill these three conditions?

What about individuality?

If we view a fetus as a "growth" within the mother's body, it would be easier to sanction her choice to remove that growth if she wishes. But a fetus is distinct from its mother from the moment of its conception.

- It is alive: it reacts to stimuli and can produce its own cells and develop them into a specific pattern of maturity.

- It is human, completely distinguishable from all other living organisms, possessing all forty-six human chromosomes, able to develop only into a human being.

- And it is complete: nothing new will be added except the growth and development of what exists from the moment of conception.

It is a scientific fact that every abortion performed in the United States is performed on a being so fully formed that its heart is beating and its brain activity can be measured on an EEG machine. At twelve weeks, the unborn baby is only about two inches long, yet every organ of the human body is clearly in place.

Theologian Karl Barth described the fetus well:

> The embryo has its own autonomy, its own brain, its own nervous system, its own blood circulation. If its life is affected by that of the mother, it also affects hers. It can have its own illnesses in which the mother has no part. Conversely, it may be quite healthy even though the mother is seriously ill. It may die while the mother continues to live. It may also continue to live after its mother's death, and be eventually saved by a timely operation on her dead body. In short, it is a human being in its own right.

And note that you did not come from a fetus–you were a fetus. A "fetus" is simply a human life in the womb. It becomes a "baby" outside the womb. But it is the same physical entity in either place. For these reasons, "pro-life" advocates believe that the U. S. Supreme Court was wrong in deciding that a fetus is not a person entitled to the full protections of the law.

Apart from spiritual or moral concerns, it is a simple fact of biology that the fetus possesses every attribute of human life we find in a newborn infant, with the exception of independent physical viability. Left unharmed, it will soon develop this capacity as well. If a life must be independently viable to be viewed as a person, a young child might well fail this standard, as would those of any age facing severe physical challenges.

WHAT DOES THE BIBLE SAY ABOUT ABORTION?

These statements are based on moral claims and legal arguments. They are intended to persuade society regardless of a person's religious persuasion. But many in our culture also want to know what the Bible says on this crucial subject.

Does the Bible talk about abortion?

The word *abortion* appears nowhere in the Bible. No one in the Bible is ever described as having an abortion, encouraging one, or even dealing with one. The Bible says nothing which specifically addresses our subject. And so many have concluded that the issue is not a biblical concern but a private matter. They say that we should be silent where the Bible is silent.

"Pro-life" advocates counter that by this logic we should be silent regarding the "Trinity" since the word never appears in Scripture. Or "marijuana" and "cocaine" since they are not in a biblical concordance. However, these issues came after the biblical era, while abortion was common in the ancient world. So this argument doesn't seem relevant.

If abortion is a biblical issue, why doesn't the Bible address it specifically? The answer is simple: the Jewish people and first Christians needed no such guidance. It was an undeniable fact of their faith and culture that abortion was wrong. How do we know? Consider early statements on the subject.

The *Sentences of Pseudo-Phocylides* is a book of Jewish wisdom written between 50 BC and AD 50. They state that "a woman should not destroy the unborn babe in her belly, nor after its birth throw it before the dogs and vultures as a prey."

The *Sibylline Oracles* are an ancient work of Jewish theology. They include among the wicked two groups: women who "produce abortions and unlawfully cast their offspring away" and sorcerers who dispense materials which cause abortions (2:339–42).

The *Mishnah* ("instruction") was the written record of Jewish oral teachings transmitted since the time of Moses. These teachings were committed to writing around 200 B.C. In the Mishnah tractate *Sanhedrin* we read: "We infer the death penalty for killing an embryo from the text, *He who sheds the blood of a man within a man, his blood shall be shed*; what is 'a man within a man'? An embryo" (Sanhedrin 57b, quoting Genesis 9:6).

An abortion was permitted only to save the life of the mother: "If a woman was in hard travail [life-threatening labor], the child must be cut up while it is in the womb and brought out member by member, since the life of the mother has priority over the life of the child; but if the great part of it was already born, it may not be touched, since the claim of one life cannot override the claim of another life" (Oholoth 7:6).

The Jews in the Old and New Testaments did not need to address the issue of abortion since no one considered it a moral option. In a similar vein, I have never preached a sermon against cigarette smoking or plagiarism. The Bible does not specifically speak to these subjects, and they are legal within certain limits, but no one in our congregation would consider them to be moral or healthy choices.

When the Christian church moved out of its Jewish context, it encountered a culture that accepted the practice of abortion. And so, after the New Testament, Christians began speaking specifically to the subject.

For instance, the *Didache* (the earliest theological treatise after the Bible) states: "You shall not procure [an] abortion, nor destroy a newborn child." And the *Epistle of Barnabas* (early second century) adds, "Thou shalt love thy neighbor more than thy own life. Thou shalt not procure abortion, thou shalt not commit infanticide." These books were widely read and accepted in the first centuries of the Christian church.

IMPORTANT BIBLICAL PASSAGES ABOUT ABORTION

While the Bible does not use the word *abortion*, it contains a number of texts that relate directly to the beginning of life and the value of all persons. Let's look briefly at the most pertinent passages.

Exodus 21:22

"Pro-choice" scholars usually begin the discussion with this statement in Exodus: "When men strive together and hit a pregnant woman, so that her children come out, but there is no harm, the one who hit her shall surely be fined, as the woman's husband shall impose on him, and he shall pay as the judges determine. But if there is harm, then you shall pay life for life, eye for eye, tooth for tooth, hand for hand, foot for foot, burn for burn, wound for wound, stripe for stripe." (Exodus 21:22–25).

In *Antiquities of the* Jews, the ancient Jewish historian Flavius Josephus commented on this text: "He that kicks a woman with child, so that the woman miscarry, let him pay a fine in money, as the judges shall determine, as having diminished the multitude by the destruction of what was in her womb; and let money also be given to the woman's husband by him that kicked her; but if she die of the stroke, let him also be put to death, the law judging it equitable that life should go for life."

But notice the translator's note: "The law seems rather to mean, that if the infant be killed, though the mother escape, the offender must be put to death; and not only when the mother is killed, as Josephus understood it."

And note this later statement by Josephus: "The law, moreover, enjoins us to bring up all our offspring, and forbids women to cause abortion of what is begotten, or to destroy it afterward; and if any woman appears to have done so, she will be a murderer of her child, by destroying a living creature, and diminishing human kind."

If this text does indeed teach that a person causing a miscarriage is only to be fined, while one causing "harm" is to receive severe punishment, we would have an important indication that the fetus is not as valuable as its mother. Is this what the text clearly teaches?

The New Revised Standard renders the text, "so that there is a miscarriage." The New American Bible Revised Edition follows suit, as does the New Jerusalem Bible. But the New International Version translates the text, "she gives birth prematurely but there is no serious injury." The New Living Translation similarly states, "they hurt a pregnant woman so that her child is born prematurely. If no further harm results . . ." The English Standard Version renders the phrase, "so that her children come out, but there is no harm." Why this crucial difference in translation?

The Hebrew phrase is literally rendered, "And they come forth children of her." "Children" is the plural of *yeled*, the usual Hebrew word for child or offspring (the Hebrew language has no separate word for "fetus" or the pre-born). "Come forth" translates *yatsa*, a word which does not specify whether the child is alive or dead, only that it leaves the womb. And so the Hebrew of Exodus 21:22 does not indicate whether the woman suffered a miscarriage (NRSV, NASB, NJB) or experienced a premature healthy birth (NIV, NLT, ESV). But it does refer to the fetus as a "child." And it is important to note that the text does not use *shachol*, the Hebrew word for "miscarriage" (this word is found in Exodus 23:26 and Hosea 9:14 among other occurrences) (For further discussion of this linguistic issue see Jack W. Cottrell's "Abortion and the Mosaic Law" in *Readings in Christian Ethics*.)

Verse 23 settles the issue for me: "But if there is serious injury . . ." (NIV), implying that no serious injury occurred in verse 22. In other words, both the mother and her child survived the attack and were healthy. And so this passage does not devalue the pre-born life or speak specifically to the issue of abortion.

Genesis 2:7

The Bible describes man's creation in this way: "These are the generations of the heavens and the earth when they were created, in the day that the Lord God made the earth and the heavens. When no bush of the field was yet in the land and no small plant of the field had yet sprung up—for the Lord God had not caused it to rain on the land, and there was no man to work the ground, and a mist was going up from the land and was watering the whole face of the ground—then the Lord God formed the man of dust from the ground and breathed into his nostrils the breath of life, and the man became a living creature" (Genesis 2:4–7).

It seems that Adam did not become a "living being" until he could breathe. And so some believe that a fetus is not a "living being" until it can breathe outside the mother's womb. Until this time it is not yet a person. President Bill Clinton explained his pro-choice position as based significantly on this logic. He said that his pastor, W. O. Vaught, former pastor of Immanuel Baptist Church in Little Rock, Arkansas, told him that this was the literal meaning of the text.

There are three problems with this argument.

1. Adam was an inanimate object until God breathed into him "the breath of life," but we know conclusively that a fetus is animate from the moment of conception.

2. The fetus breathes in the womb, exchanging amniotic fluid for air after birth.

3. Adam in Genesis 2:7 was a potential life even before he became a human being. By any definition, a fetus is at the very least a potential human being. We'll say more about this fact in a moment.

Psalm 139

One of David's best-loved psalms contains this affirmation: "For you formed my inward parts; you knitted me together in my mother's womb. I praise you, for I am fearfully and wonderfully made. Wonderful are your works; my soul knows it very well. My frame was not hidden from you, when I was being made in secret, intricately woven in the depths of the earth. Your eyes saw my unformed substance; in your book were written, every one of them, the days that were formed for me, when as yet there was none of them" (Psalm 139:13–16).

David clearly believed that God created him in his mother's womb and "beheld my unformed substance" before he was born. "Pro-life" theologians point to this declaration as proof that life is created by God and begins at conception.

Of course, those who do not accept the authority of Scripture will not be persuaded by this argument. And some who do believe that David's statement is poetic symbolism rather than scientific description. He is simply stating that he is God's creation, without speaking specifically to the status of a fetus.

Jeremiah 1:5

As part of God's call to the prophet Jeremiah, the Lord issued this declaration: "Before I formed you in the womb I knew you, and before you were born I consecrated you; I appointed you a prophet to the nations" (Jeremiah 1:5). God clearly formed Jeremiah in the womb and "knew" him even before that time. He "consecrated" or called him to special service even before he was born. God's plan for Jeremiah began before his conception and his birth.

It's hard for me to see how those who accept biblical authority could make a "pro-choice" response to this statement. I suppose they could claim that the verse is symbolic and spiritual, not scientific, that it is a metaphorical description of God's eternal plan for Jeremiah. But the text seems to be specifically related to Jeremiah's conception and gestation.

Luke 1:39–45

Luke's gospel records the visit of the pregnant Mary to the pregnant Elizabeth: "In those days Mary set out and went with haste to a Judean town in the hill country, where she entered the house of Zechariah and greeted Elizabeth.

When Elizabeth heard Mary's greeting, the child leaped in her womb. And Elizabeth was filled with the Holy Spirit and exclaimed with a loud cry, "Blessed are you among women, and blessed is the fruit of your womb! And why is this granted to me, that the mother of my Lord should come to me? For behold, when the sound of your greeting came to my ears, the baby in my womb leaped for joy. And blessed is she who believed that there would be a fulfillment of what was spoken to her from the Lord" (Luke 1:42–45).

When Elizabeth said that "the baby in my womb leaped for joy" (v. 44), she made clear the fact that her "fetus" was a fully responding being. She used the word *brephos,* the Greek term for baby, embryo, fetus, newborn child, young child, or nursing child. It is the same word used to describe Jesus in the manger, where the shepherds "went with haste and found Mary and Joseph, and the *baby* lying in the manger" (Luke 2:16).

Paul used the word in reminding Timothy "how from *childhood* you have known the sacred writings that are able to instruct you for salvation through faith in Christ Jesus" (2 Timothy 3:15). The Bible makes no linguistic distinction between the personhood of a human being, whether before or after its birth.

What are the rights of the innocent?

The Bible consistently defends the rights of those who are innocent and undeserving of punishment or death. For instance:

- "Do not kill the innocent and righteous, for I will not acquit the guilty" (Exodus 23:7).

- "There are six things that the Lord hates, seven that are an abomination to him: haughty eyes, a lying tongue, and hands that shed innocent blood, a heart that devises wicked plans, feet that make haste to run to evil, a false witness who breathes out lies, and one who sows discord among brothers" (Proverbs 6:16–19).

- The Babylonians attacked Jerusalem "for the sins of Manasseh, according to all that he had done, and also for the innocent blood that he had shed. For he filled Jerusalem with innocent blood, and the Lord would not pardon" (2 Kings 24:3–4).

It is clear that God cares for the innocent and defenseless of the world. Children, whether before their birth or after, would be among his most valued creations.

How have Christians viewed abortion?

How has the Church viewed the issue of abortion across its history? Are "pro-choice" religious leaders in step with traditional Christian thinking on this subject? Or has the Church even spoken with a unified voice when addressing the question?

Early church fathers were clear in their opposition to abortion.

Athenagoras (ca. AD 150), Clement of Alexandria (ca. 150–215), Tertullian (ca. 155–225), St. Hippolytus (ca. 170–236), St. Basil the Great (ca. 330–79), St. Ambrose (ca. 339–97), St. John Chrysostom (ca. 340–407), and St. Jerome (ca. 342–420) all issued strong condemnations of this practice.

However, these theologians did not specifically say when the body receives a soul. This is the process called "animation" or "ensoulment" by early philosophers. Many in the ancient world followed the thinking of Aristotle (384–322 BC) on the issue. He believed that "ensoulment" occurred forty days after conception in males and ninety days in females, and taught that abortion prior to this time was not murder.

St. Augustine of Hippo (354–430), arguably the greatest theological mind after Paul, can be quoted on both sides of the issue. As regards whether souls are given to bodies at conception, Augustine said in Book I of *On the Soul and its Origin*, "He . . . who formed them, knows whether He formed them with the soul, or gave the soul to them after they had been formed. . . . I have no certain knowledge how it came into my body; for it was not I who gave it to myself." He was critical of a theologian who was too dogmatic on this issue, claiming, "how much better it is for him to share my hesitation about the soul's origin." He did not believe that we can know when people "obtain their souls."

And yet Augustine was convinced that those who die in the womb will be resurrected with the rest of humanity and given perfect bodies in heaven. If they died, they must have lived; if they lived, they will be resurrected. Babies deformed at birth will be given perfect bodies in paradise as well (*Enchiridion* 85). It would seem that Augustine believed life to begin at conception, as the moment the fetus can die, it must have been alive.

Theologians, popes, and church councils in the centuries to follow would continue to debate this issue. St. Jerome (ca. 342–420) could speak of the "murder of an unborn child" (Letter 22:13), and yet he could state that abortion is not killing until the fetus acquires limbs and shape (Letter 121:4). Pope Innocent III (ca. 1161–1216) stated that the soul enters the body of the fetus when the woman feels the first movement of the fetus (the "quickening"). After such "ensoulment," abortion is murder; previously it is a less serious sin, as it ends only potential human life.

Thomas Aquinas (1225?–74) condemned abortion for any and all reasons. However, he agreed with Aristotle's conclusion that a male child was formed enough to be judged human at forty days, a female at eighty. Only when the fetus could be considered human could it have a soul.

On the other hand, Pope Leo XIII (1878–1903) issued a decree in 1886 that prohibited all procedures which directly kill the fetus, even to save the life of the mother. He also required excommunication for abortions at any stage of pregnancy.

To summarize, Christian leaders across church history have been uniform in their condemnation of abortion once the fetus was considered to be a "person."

Many in the ancient and medieval world were influenced by Aristotle's beliefs regarding the time when this occurred. If they could know what we know about the fetus from its earliest stages of life, I believe they would revise their opinion and condemn abortion from the moment of conception. But it is impossible to know their position on information they did not possess.

WHAT ABOUT RAPE AND INCEST?

The Bible makes rape a capital offense: "If the man meets the engaged woman in the open country, and the man seizes her and lies with her, then only the man who lay with her shall die. You shall do nothing to the young woman; the young woman has not committed an offense punishable by death, because this case is like that of someone who attacks and murders a neighbor" (Deuteronomy 22:25–26).

God's word clearly condemns such a crime against women.

"Pro-choice" advocates often point to this issue early in the debate, arguing that a woman should not continue to be victimized by bearing a child as the result of such a horrific crime.

Unprotected intercourse results in pregnancy about four percent of the time. If one in three women is likely to be raped in her lifetime, and incestuous relationships subject a woman to repeated sexual abuse, pregnancies resulting from rape and incest are so likely that abortion must be legal as a remedy for women subjected to such crime. Nearly all pro-life advocates concede the point, allowing for abortion in the case of rape and incest.

However, it has been established by numerous surveys over the years that rape and incest victims represent approximately one percent of the abortion cases recorded annually in this country. A decision to limit abortions to this exception would prevent the deaths of nearly all of the 1.5 million babies who are aborted each year. Only about three percent of the abortions performed each year in America relate to the health of the mother, and three percent relate to the health of the child. Ninety-three percent are elective.

To allow for abortion because of the very rare incidence of abortions performed because of rape and incest is something like suspending all marijuana laws because of the small number of patients who could benefit from its medicinal effects. We could stop the use of traffic lights because of the incidents when they slow a sick person's rush to a hospital, but would we not cause more harm than we prevent?

At the same time, Americans must be conscious of the fact that rape and incest are far more common in some other countries and cultures. Rape in particular is a typical means of coercion and military control in some societies. There the percentage of abortions related to rape may be much higher than is the case in America.

This caveat stated, I'm not sure that even this decision is the moral choice. I must quickly admit that my status as an American, Anglo male makes it very difficult for me to commiserate with women who have experienced such trauma as rape and incest. But it is hard for me to understand how the child which is produced by this terrible crime does not deserve to live. Ethel Waters, the famous gospel singer, was the product of a rape. So was a student I taught at Southwestern Seminary, an evangelist with a global ministry today. I tread very lightly here, but would at the very least suggest that this issue is far from the primary cause of abortion in America today.

A WAY FORWARD IN PRO-LIFE VS. PRO-CHOICE

"Pro-life" advocates typically believe that life begins at conception, so that abortion is wrong. "Pro-choice" advocates typically believe that life begins when the fetus is viable independent of its mother or at birth, and that abortion should be a legal choice for the mother prior to that point. The framers of the Constitution did not address this issue. The Supreme Court in 1973 interpreted this silence to mean that constitutional rights to life do not extend to the pre-born. And yet the Bible speaks with a single voice in viewing the pre-born as the creation of God and as children deserving of protection and care.

In light of these contradictory facts, is there a way to move forward?

Given that the participants in this debate come from a variety of religious and personal worldviews, it seems implausible to find common ground by beginning with biblical teachings or religious convictions. So I suggest the following non-religious, constitutional strategy.

First, we should build a consensus for permitting abortion to protect the life of the mother or in cases of rape and incest.

These account for a small percentage of the 1.5 million abortions performed each year. Even though some (like me) question the morality of this position, most would concede the point in order to reduce the 93 percent of abortions which are elective in nature. Allowing for this exception removes the most obvious and emotional obstacle to the "pro-life" position.

Second, we should understand that the pre-born possess at least the potential for "life," however it is defined.

Many of us believe that a fetus is a human being by every definition of the term except independent viability, and note that the pre-born will attain this status unless harmed. But even those who disagree with this assertion will admit that every fetus is in the process of becoming a "person."

Third, "pro-life" and "pro-choice" advocates should work together to fulfill President Clinton's desire that abortion be "rare."

Even the most ardent "pro-choice" supporters surely would support an agenda intended to decrease the number of abortions performed each year. One way to achieve this goal would be for both sides to promote adoption as the best answer to an unwanted pregnancy. Both sides could also support abstinence and birth control education. Many "pro-life" advocates view birth control measures as promoting sexual promiscuity, but we may have to choose between sexual activity or unintended pregnancy and a resulting abortion.

Both sides could join forces in educating the public about the actual characteristics of the fetus. It has been proven that women are far less likely to choose abortion when they see a sonogram of their unborn child or learn about its present capacities. Adoption would then become a more likely option for the mother to choose. Leaders from both sides could be asked to adopt a united agenda aimed at decreasing the number of abortions performed each year in our country. If this strategy is successful, it may change the public's opinion regarding the morality of abortion.

Fourth, whatever the "pro-choice" position decides to do to help limit abortions, "pro-life" advocates must do all we can to care for both the unborn child and its mother.

We must care for the mother and the father of the child, and do all we can to help those who have chosen abortion in the past. We must work hard to advocate adoption and to provide life necessities for at-risk families. We must be "pro-life," not just "pro-birth."

It may be that these steps would eventually help to change the legal status of abortion. A constitutional amendment extending legal protection to the fetus would be more likely to pass if more Americans were taught to view the fetus as a life. Alternately, it would be more likely that the courts would recognize the rising consensus against abortion and rule in light of this conventional wisdom.

CHOOSE LIFE

Mother Teresa, writing to the US Supreme Court as it was considering petitions related to the abortion issue, stated boldly:

> Your opinion [in Roe v. Wade] stated that you did not need to "resolve the difficult question of when life begins." That question is inescapable. If the right to life is an inherent and inalienable right, it must surely obtain wherever human life exists. No one can deny that the unborn child is a distinct being, that it is human, and that it is alive. It is unjust, therefore, to deprive the unborn child of its fundamental right to life on the basis of its age, size, or condition of dependency. It was a sad infidelity to America's highest ideals when this Court said that it did not matter, or could not be determined, when the inalienable right to life began for a child in its mother's womb.

She has been widely quoted as stating, "It is a poverty to decide that a child must die so that you may live as you wish."

I attended my first National Prayer Breakfast in 1995, where I heard remarkable speakers address the president and other national leaders. Those attending were still talking about the previous year's keynote speaker. Mother Teresa, eighty-three years old in 1994, had said to the three thousand in the audience, "I feel that the greatest destroyer of peace today is abortion, because it is a war against the child, a direct killing of the innocent child, murder by the mother herself. And if we accept that a mother can kill even her own child, how can we tell other people not to kill one another?" Later in her speech, she implored the gathering, "Please don't kill the child. I want the child. Please give me the child." She received a standing ovation. After her speech, she approached President Clinton, pointed her finger at him, and said, "Stop killing babies."

Would abortion be a moral choice when a family is very, very poor—when they have fourteen children and another on the way? That child was John Wesley. What about a father who is ill and a mother with tuberculosis? Their first child is blind, the second is deceased, the third is deaf, and the fourth has tuberculosis. Now she is pregnant again. Her son would be called Beethoven. A white man rapes a thirteen-year-old black girl and she becomes pregnant. Her child is Ethel Waters. A teenage girl is pregnant, but her fiancée is not the father of the baby. Her baby is Jesus.

In a church I once pastored, a woman gave me her unsolicited testimony regarding an abortion she had chosen eleven years earlier. Here's her story:

> I cried tears of shame, tears of pain, tears
> of heartache. I cried for my sin so black I
> didn't believe that there could ever be a way
> that I could make amends–ever be a way
> that I could atone for what I had done. That
> there could ever be a way that I could be
> clean again. For 11 years I cried for myself,
> because I couldn't get away from what I had
> done.
>
> But God blessed me. In the depths of my
> dark and lonely valley he was there. His
> grace and mercy are great–his love is so
> wonderful. He wooed me back to his side,
> saying to me, My child, my child, I love you.

O my child I love you. Yes, I forgive you.

I am blessed. I know that I am forgiven. I have forgiven myself–God has healed me. But many are not so blessed–they never get to meet my Jesus; they never experience his love and forgiveness. For them, the crying goes on.

A DISCUSSION GUIDE ON ABORTION

The following discussion guide may be used in a small group setting or for your personal time of devotion. We hope it helps you both better understand the topic and how God might want to use you, in your specific context, to be "salt and light" on this issue. A PDF download is available at denisonforum.org/courage-questions.

1. What is your stance on abortion? What views does your local community hold on abortion?

2. Review the following statistics:

    •   "Every year, more than thirty-six thousand people die on US highways. Every sixteen days, that many abortions are performed in America."

    •   "Since the Supreme Court's Roe v. Wade decision legalized abortion in 1973, more than sixty-one million abortions have been performed in America."

Before reading this article, were you familiar with the US abortion rate? What does this tell us about the reality of abortion in our country?

3. I state that "abortion is the moral issue of our time." Do you agree? Why or why not?

4. Review the four arguments that have developed since 1973 regarding when abortion should be permissible.

- There should be no right to an abortion, even to save the life of the mother. This has been the Catholic Church's usual position.

- Therapeutic abortions can be performed to save the mother's life.

- Extreme case abortions can be permitted in cases of rape, incest, or severe deformation of the fetus. Most pro-life advocates would accept therapeutic and extreme case abortions.

- Abortion should be available to any woman who chooses it.

Which of the statements seems most reasonable and why?

5. Review the five moral arguments for pro-choice:

- No one can say when a fetus becomes a person, so the mother is the most appropriate person to make decisions regarding it.

- Abortion must be protected so a woman who is the victim of rape or incest does not have to bear a child resulting from such an attack.

- No unwanted child should be brought into the world.

- The state has no right to legislate personal morality.

- A woman must be permitted to make pregnancy decisions in light of her life circumstances.

Have you ever entered into a discussion or debate with someone regarding these statements? If so, how did you respond? I expound on the five arguments. To what extent do you empathize with my reasoning?

6. Read the following pro-life arguments listed in the article.

   • A fetus is a human life and should be granted the full protection of the law.

   • Most pro-life advocates are willing to permit abortion in cases of rape or incest or to protect the life of the mother.

   • Pro-life advocates agree that all children should be wanted, so they argue strongly for adoption as an alternative to abortion.

   • Pro-life supporters do not see abortion legislation as an intrusion into areas of private morality.

   • Pro-life advocates want to encourage the health of both the mother and the child and do not believe that we must choose between the two.

Does one argument stand out to you as particularly significant? If so, why? Do you disagree with any of the statements? Do Christians act honorably when standing for these principles? If so, how? If not, how can Christian communities better show their pro-life support?

7. Consider the following approaches to the question "When does life begin"?

   • **Functionalism**: A fetus is a "person" when it can act personally as a moral, intellectual, and spiritual agent.

   • **Actualism**: A fetus is a person if it possesses the potential for developing self-conscious, personal life. This definition would permit abortion when the fetus clearly does not possess the capacity for functional life.

- **Essentialism**: A fetus is a person from conception, whatever its health or potential. It is an individual in the earliest stages of development and deserves all the protections afforded to other persons by our society.

Which approach seems most biblical? Why?

8. Why is our answer as Christians to the question "When does life begin?" so important?

9. What Christian teaching have you heard on abortion? Do these use specific Bible passages? If so, which ones?

10. Of the important passages highlighted in this essay, which for you best explains the biblical stance of life in the womb? (Exodus 21:22, Genesis 2:7, Psalm 139, Jeremiah 1:5, Luke 1:39–45). Which of these passages is most shocking to you, if any?

11. Do you think that mothers who have been raped should be able to opt for abortion? If so, why?

12. In "A way forward in pro-life vs. pro-choice," I write that Christians should:

- One: build a consensus for permitting abortion to protect the life of the mother or in cases of rape and incest.

- Two: understand that the pre-born possess at least the potential for "life," however it is defined.

- Three: "Pro-life" and "pro-choice" advocates should

work together to fulfill President Clinton's desire that abortion be "rare."

- Four: whatever the "pro-choice" position decides to do to help limit abortions, "pro-life" advocates must do all we can to care for both the unborn child and its mother.

Are the points straightforward, or is there room for disagreement? Which of the points resonated most with you? Are there any you would add to the list?

13. Reread the testimony given at the end of the article. In our local communities, how can we better serve women considering abortion or women who have already had one?

14. Does knowing that so many of the "greats" in history were unwanted pregnancies shift your perspective on abortion?

15. Have any of your views been changed or altered after reading this article? If so, how?

CHAPTER 3

THE CALL TO TRANSFORMATIONAL GOOD:
What does the Bible say about politics?

William Wilberforce experienced a spiritual rebirth on Easter 1786 that led him to discover his life's purpose. As he wrote later in his diary, "My walk is a public one. My business is in the world, and I must mix in the assemblies of men or quit the post which Providence seems to have assigned me."

He soon came to see the horrors of the English slave trade and became so convicted that he wrote, "Let the consequences be what they would: I from this time determined that I would never rest until I had effected its absolution." He was vilified by pro-slavery forces and blocked repeatedly in Parliament. However, the persistent and sacrificial efforts of Wilberforce and his associates finally led to the abolishing of the slave trade and slavery in the British Empire. Historian G. M. Trevelyan later called this "one of the turning events in the history of the world." As Wilberforce's story illustrates, God can use Christians in politics for profound and transformational good.

Merriam-Webster defines "politics" as "the art or science of government." The word comes from the Greek *polis*, meaning "city." It has its roots in Aristotle's classic work, *Politika*, which introduced the Greek term *politika*, meaning "affairs of the cities."

Anthropologists generally recognize four kinds of political systems:

1. **The band**: a small family group consisting of no more than thirty to fifty individuals.

2. **The tribe**: a group consisting of many families with social institutions such as chiefs or elders. They are more permanent than bands.

3. **The chiefdom**: more complex than a tribe or a band society, they have a centralized authority structure and institutional leadership.

4. **The sovereign state**: a state with a permanent population, a defined territory, a government, and the capacity to relate to other sovereign states.

For the purposes of this chapter, we will focus on biblical insights with regard to the "sovereign state" of the United States. What insights can help Christians relate more effectively to our culture as salt and light? How can we make a difference in the culture and act in ways that empower our witness?

Let's consider three biblical facts.

ONE: GOD CALLS AND USES POLITICAL LEADERS

In *Nicomachean Ethics*, Aristotle observed, "Politicians have no leisure, because they are always aiming at something beyond political life itself, power and glory, or happiness." Russian Premier Nikita Khrushchev made a similar point: "Politicians are the same all over. They promise to build a bridge even where there is no river."

It is tempting for Christians to stay "above" politics and out of the fray. In this day of "cancel culture" and 24/7 media coverage, in a nation that feels more divided and divisive than ever, it is understandable for good people to sit on the sidelines. However, as Plato noted in *The Republic*, "One of the penalties for refusing to participate in politics is that you end up being governed by your inferiors." The Bible makes clear that, despite the stigma often associated with politics, God calls and uses political leaders. Consider three dimensions of this call.

God uses leaders who partner with him

The Bible is replete with stories of political leaders called and used by God to work with him in advancing his kingdom on earth. Let's review four such examples.

One: Joseph

Joseph was sold into slavery by his brothers at the age of seventeen. Thirteen years later, he became what we might call the "prime minister" of Egypt, the world's greatest superpower. His rise to power was no accident: When he was in prison, God gave him the ability to interpret

Pharaoh's dreams, thus predicting seven years of plenty followed by seven years of famine (Genesis 41:1–36). As a result, "Pharaoh said to his servants, 'Can we find a man like this, in whom is the Spirit of God?'" (v. 38).

Pharaoh then appointed Joseph to political office: "You shall be over my house, and all my people shall order themselves as you command. Only as regards the throne will I be greater than you" (v. 40). This description means Joseph was appointed as the "grand vizier" of Egypt. In this role, he was instrumental in saving the Egyptian people and his own family from starvation, preserving the Jewish nation through whom the Messiah would come one day.

Two: Israel's leaders

God called Moses to lead his people out of Egyptian slavery (Exodus 3) and then Joshua to follow next (Joshua 1:1–2). The Lord then "raised up judges, who saved [the nation] out of the hand of those who plundered them" (Judges 2:16). God later designated Saul to be Israel's first king (1 Samuel 9:15–17) and David to be his successor (1 Samuel 16:12–13).

Three: Mordecai

The book of Esther tells us about the plot of Haman against God's people in Persia. After this nefarious plot was exposed, "the king took off his signet ring, which he had taken from Haman, and gave it to Mordecai" (Esther 8:2). This action advanced Mordecai to the position of first minister of the king with authority akin to that of Joseph centuries earlier.

As a result, "Mordecai went out from the presence of the king in royal robes of blue and white, and with a great golden crown and a robe of fine linen and purple" (v. 15).

Soon "the fear of Mordecai" fell on "all the officials of the provinces and the satraps and the governors and the royal agents" of the land (Esther 9:3). This was because "Mordecai was great in the king's house, and his fame spread throughout all the provinces, for the man Mordecai grew more and more powerful" (v. 4). Consequently, Mordecai's leadership enabled the Jews to defend themselves from their enemies, again preserving the nation through whom the Messiah would come.

Four: Daniel and his friends

Daniel and his friends were Jewish exiles in Babylon. Scripture says that "God gave them learning and skill in all literature and wisdom, and Daniel had understanding in all visions and dreams" (Daniel 1:17). As a result, the king elevated them to positions of political authority. Then, when Daniel (like Joseph) interpreted the king's dreams, "the king gave Daniel high honors and many great gifts, and made him ruler over the whole province of Babylon and chief prefect over all the wise men of Babylon" (Daniel 2:48).

Clearly, God calls some people into political service. We see this fact not only in Scripture but across history as well.

According to Pew Research Center, nearly all US presidents have been identified with the Christian faith. Eleven were Episcopalian; nine were Presbyterian; four were Baptist; four were Unitarian; three were Methodist; three were members of the Christian church; two were members of the Disciples of Christ; two were Dutch Reformed; two were Quaker; one was Catholic; and one was a Congregationalist. Only Thomas Jefferson and Abraham Lincoln had no formal church affiliation.

William Wilberforce's Christian faith led him to fight within Parliament for the abolition of the slave trade in England. Presbyterian minister John Witherspoon was the only active clergyman to sign the Declaration of Independence. Dr. Martin Luther King Jr. was a Baptist minister before he assumed political leadership of the civil rights movement.

It is clear that God calls some people into political service and uses them in this role.

God uses leaders who oppose him

Generations after Joseph's death, another Pharaoh who saw the Jewish people as a threat rose to power (Exodus 1:8–12) and "ruthlessly made the people of Israel work as slaves" (v. 13). In response, God raised up Moses to oppose Pharaoh and free his people from slavery. God then used Pharaoh's "hardened heart" to bring about the Exodus. As a result, "Israel saw the great power that the Lord used against the Egyptians, so the people feared the Lord, and they believed in the Lord and in his servant Moses" (Exodus 14:31).
The Lord used King Herod's attempt to murder the baby Jesus to fulfill biblical prophecy regarding his Son's flight to Egypt (Matthew 2:13–15). He likewise used opposition from Jewish authorities in Jerusalem to bring his Son to the cross as our Savior.

After Roman magistrates in Philippi gave orders for Paul and Silas to be beaten and imprisoned (Acts 16:22–24), God redeemed their suffering by leading their jailer and his family to Christ (vv. 25–34). The Lord used opposition from a Roman government official to bring Paul to Rome (Acts 25:12). He used Rome's exile of John to Patmos to give us the book of Revelation (cf. Revelation 1:9).

As a contemporary example, Christianity has exploded in China in the decades after Communist leaders took over in 1949. Today, China is the world's largest producer of Bibles. There are more Christians than members of the Communist Party in China. According to one scholar, "On any given Sunday, there are almost certainly more Protestants in church in China than in all of Europe."

And no one knows with certainty the size of the "underground" church in China. When I was in Beijing several years ago, I met with a group of pastors who serve such congregations. Their stories about divine protection and evangelistic multiplication read like the book of Acts.

I have been privileged to travel to Cuba ten times over the years. The spiritual awakening occurring in this Communist country is truly inspiring. On my first visit, I told one of the Cuban pastors that I was sorry for the persecution he and his people were facing and that I was praying for such opposition to lessen. He asked me not to continue with such intercession, explaining that persecution was strengthening his people and purifying their faith. Then he added that he and many other Cubans were praying for persecution to increase in the US for the same reasons.

God uses leaders who don't know they are being used

The Persian king under whom Mordecai served issued an edict stating that "the king allowed the Jews who were in every city to gather and defend their lives, to destroy, to kill, and to annihilate any armed force of any people or province that might attack them" (Esther 8:11). We have no biblical evidence that the king knew he was working to preserve God's chosen people through whom our Savior would come, but he was.

When Paul's enemies brought him before the court in Corinth, the proconsul Gallio set him free, enabling the apostle's continued ministry (Acts 18:12–16). When a riot led by idolaters broke out in Ephesus, "some of the Asiarchs, who were friends of [Paul's], sent to him and were urging him not to venture into the theater" (Acts 19:31). The "Asiarchs" were custodians of the imperial Roman cult in Asia and people of high political rank. The crowd dragged Gaius and Aristarchus, Paul's traveling companions, into the theater. However, the "town clerk" (the chief administrative officer in Ephesus) "quieted the crowd" and persuaded them to disperse (vv. 35, 41).

When Paul returned to Jerusalem, another riot broke out. However, "the tribune of the cohort" intervened (Acts 21:31). He was commander of a thousand soldiers and a person of significant authority in the city. He preserved Paul's life and enabled the furtherance of his ministry. The Jewish authorities then plotted to take Paul's life, but his nephew warned him and then brought word to the tribune. This official then provided protection for Paul and sent him along with an explanatory letter to Felix the governor in Caesarea (Acts 23:17–35).

Felix later heard Paul's case and refused to turn him over to his adversaries (Acts 24:22–23). His successor, Festus, refused a request for Paul to be returned to Jerusalem, not knowing that his enemies "were planning an ambush to kill him on the way" (Acts 25:3). Festus then honored Paul's appeal to Caesar and provided him transportation and security to Rome (Acts 27:1).

The Bible teaches that "the king's heart is a stream of water in the hand of the Lord; he turns it wherever he will" (Proverbs 21:1). No matter what circumstances seem to say, "kingship belongs to the Lord, and he rules over the nations" (Psalm 22:28). As a result, we can know that God is using leaders whether they know they are being used or not. John Calvin was right: "It is a most blessed thing to be subject to the sovereignty of God."

TWO: GOD IS CALLING US TO PARTICIPATE IN POLITICS

I have been privileged over the years to know several Christians in political leadership, both as their pastor and as their friend. One of the frequent concerns I have heard them express is the common misperception that Christians have done all they need to do if they elect Christians to office. The fact is, voting is vital, but it is just the beginning of our biblical responsibility with regard to politics.

It is true that "our citizenship is in heaven" (Philippians 3:20), but it is also true that we are to be good stewards of our time on earth. The Lord told his exiled people in Babylon: "Build houses and live in them; plant gardens and eat their produce. Take wives and have sons and daughters; take wives for your sons, and give your daughters in marriage, that they may bear sons and daughters; multiply there, and do not decrease. But seek the welfare of the city where I have sent you into exile, and pray to the Lord on its behalf, for in its welfare you will find your welfare" (Jeremiah 29:5–7).

As the "salt of the earth" and the "light of the world" (Matthew 5:13–14), the flourishing of our world is, in part, our responsibility. If I have the only light in a dark room, its darkness is my fault. Caring for our culture and engaging in its political processes is part of good citizenship for God's people.

To that end, consider four practical imperatives for Christians.

Vote

Voting is an essential responsibility for all Americans and for all Christians. We should learn all we can about the candidates and their positions, especially in the context of biblical principles. We should ask God to guide us in casting our ballots. The Voting Assistance Center at MyFaithVotes. org offers a wealth of helpful resources to this end, covering federal, state, and local candidates. And we should encourage everyone we can to vote as well.

How are you preparing now for your next federal, state, or local election?

Engage with legislators

One of the values of representative democracy is the degree to which our leaders are responsible to those who elect them. Several political leaders have shared with me the fact that even a few citizens who make their views known on pending legislation can make an enormous difference.

- Contact your congressional representatives. Note: it is best to speak to them or their aides personally rather than sending emails or leaving voice mails that can be ignored.

- Go to meetings organized by leaders in your community.

- Organize groups to speak with your representatives about issues important to you.

- Volunteer for candidates and causes by knocking on doors, making fundraising calls, and organizing voter registration drives.

Are you asking God to show you if and how he wants you to be involved personally in our political process?

Serve in public office

As we have seen, God calls men and women into political service and uses their work for his glory and our good. I am convinced, in fact, that God is calling more Christians into public service today than are answering his call.

Have you asked God if he is calling you into such service?

Intercede

Paul's word to Timothy is God's word to us: "I urge that supplications, prayers, intercessions, and thanksgivings be made for all people, for kings and all who are in high positions" (1 Timothy 2:1–2). We are to pray for our leaders whether we agree with them or not; in fact, the less we agree, the more we should intercede. We should pray not just for the president and national leaders but for state and local leaders as well. Do you know the names of your city council? Are you praying for them and for your mayor? For your governor and state officials? For the president and his cabinet?

THREE: WE MUST SERVE OUR HIGHEST AUTHORITY

A survey of biblical teaching with regard to politics would not be complete without a fuller discussion of religious liberty, which is the topic of our next chapter. For now, we must note that while Scripture calls us to honor and respect the authorities he institutes (Romans 13:1), if forced to choose we should echo the apostles: "We must obey God rather than men" (Acts 5:29).

Such a choice will often come with consequences—and part of obeying God rather than men involves a willingness to accept those consequences when necessary—but the price for choosing to make anyone or anything a higher authority in our life than God is much higher in the end.

CONCLUSION

George Washington stated in his Farewell Address, "The propitious smiles of heaven can never be expected on a nation that disregards the eternal rules of order and right which heaven itself has ordained." What if the spiritual future of our country depended upon the degree to which God's people incarnate and advance "the eternal rules of order and right" in our day?

It does.

A DISCUSSION GUIDE ON POLITICS

The following discussion guide may be used in a small group setting or for your personal time of devotion. We hope it helps you both better understand the topic and how God might want to use you, in your specific context, to be "salt and light" on this issue. A PDF download is available at denisonforum.org/courage-questions.

1. Do you consider yourself a political person? Why or why not?

2. Do you think the Bible addresses politics? If so, how?

3. How did God use political leaders in the Bible?

4. Outside of the examples listed in the article, what other political leaders did God use in the Bible?

5. How does God use political leaders today?

6. Why does the church seem to flourish when it's persecuted?

7. Read Psalm 22:28. How does that apply to who rules you? To you?

8. How have you prepared yourself, either now or in the past, for upcoming presidential voting days?

9. How can a Christian discern if God is calling them to serve in public office? (Alternately, why should more Christians consider lives of public service?)

10. 1Of the four ways listed to engage in politics, which do you routinely do? Why? Which do you fail to do? Why? What other ways might a Christian engage in the political process?

11. Is it ever **OK** for a Christian to disobey the government? If so, what should be taken into account?

12. How will God's word shape your politics going forward?

CHAPTER 4

THE OPPORTUNITY TO ENGAGE CULTURE:
What does the Bible say about religious liberty?

Are Christians facing "a hill to die on"? This idiom has been explained: "Fighting to take the position of a hill from an enemy is nearly impossible and results in mass casualties. One must be sure that the hill is worth the cost of taking it." Colonial Americans determined that freedom from the oppression of Britain was such a hill. America's leaders determined that responding to the Japanese attack on Pearl Harbor and jihadist terrorism on 9/11 were such hills.

Are America's Christians facing threats to our religious liberty on such a level that we must stand up at any cost? Have we reached that point where we must say to secular authorities, "We must obey God rather than men" (Acts 5:29)?

PUBLIC WORSHIP AND GOVERNMENTAL AUTHORITY

In 2020, three churches in California filed a federal lawsuit against Gov. Gavin Newsom, claiming that a ban on singing in worship to help stem the spread of coronavirus violated their First Amendment rights. One explained, "Singing in church is a biblical mandate." They pointed to the governor's support of Black Lives Matter protests, claiming that he protected the protesters' freedom of expression while blocking that of Christians in worship. In their view, the governor's act constitutes a breach of their religious freedom.

John MacArthur's well-known church in the Los Angeles area chose to reopen for in-person worship; a video of his sermon showed attendees sitting beside each other without wearing masks. The church's website defended the decision as obeying "the biblical mandate to gather for corporate worship."

South Bay United Pentecostal Church v. Newsom

In late May 2020, in *South Bay United Pentecostal Church v. Newsom,* the US Supreme Court denied a California church's request for an injunction against the state's phased reopening plan. The governor's executive order limited religious gatherings to 25 percent of building capacity or a maximum of one hundred attendees. The court determined by a five-to-four vote that "although California's guidelines place restrictions on places of worship, those restrictions appear consistent with the Free Exercise Clause of the First Amendment. Similar or more severe restrictions apply to comparable secular gatherings, including lectures, concerts, movie showings, spectator sports, and theatrical performances, where large groups of people gather in close proximity for extended periods of time."

By contrast, the majority noted, "the Order exempts or treats more leniently only dissimilar activities, such as operating grocery stores, banks, and laundromats, in which people neither congregate in large groups nor remain in close proximity for extended periods." Writing in dissent, Justice Kavanaugh disagreed: "California's 25 percent occupancy cap on religious worship services indisputably discriminates against religion, and such discrimination violates the First Amendment." His dissent was joined by Justice Thomas and Justice Gorsuch.

We can view this case as a disagreement regarding which activities are more like attending worship services and therefore subject to California's attendance cap, or we can see it as an attack on public worship and therefore on religious liberty.

Calvary Chapel Dayton Valley v. Sisolak

Another Supreme Court case caused grave concern. In *Calvary Chapel Dayton Valley v. Sisolak*, the same five-to-four majority denied a request from a Nevada church that it be allowed to operate under the same conditions as similar secular businesses. The church wanted to hold services at 50 percent capacity rather than having the state cap its attendance at fifty people regardless of the size of the church building. Restaurants, bars, gyms, and casinos operate under the more permissive 50 percent capacity rule.

In his dissent, Justice Gorsuch states: "There is no world in which the Constitution permits Nevada to favor Caesars Palace over Calvary Chapel." Justice Kavanaugh also dissented, stating: "Unlike a casino next door, a church with a 500-person occupancy limit may let in only 50 people, not 250 people. Nevada has offered no persuasive justification for that overt discrimination against places of worship.

The risk of COVID-19 transmission is at least as high at restaurants, bars, casinos, and gyms as it is at religious services. Indeed, people congregating in restaurants, bars, casinos, and gyms often linger at least as long as they do at religious services."

He added: "To be clear, a State's closing or reopening plan may subject religious organizations to the *same* limits as secular organizations. And in light of the devastating COVID-19 pandemic, those limits may be very strict. But a State may not impose strict limits on places of worship and looser limits on restaurants, bars, casinos, and gyms, at least without sufficient justification for the differential treatment of religion" (his emphasis). He stated that "the State has not explained" why the 50 percent occupancy cap "is good enough for secular businesses where people congregate in large groups or remain in close proximity for extended periods—such as at restaurants, bars, casinos, and gyms—but is not good enough for places of worship."

Nevada apparently did not provide such justification to the court. However, some argued that church services were uniquely dangerous with regard to spreading the SARS-CoV-2 virus. Carlos del Rio, an infectious disease expert at Emory University, said of church gatherings, "It's an ideal setting for transmission. You have a lot of people in a closed space. And they're speaking loudly, they're singing. All those things are exactly what you don't want." By mid-July 2020, more than 650 cases of COVID-19 had been linked to religious facilities.

Health experts warned that singing in public was especially dangerous, noting that singers use "diaphragmatic breathing" that generates a greater number of aerosols and spreads them a long distance. One choir in Washington had an outbreak in which fifty-two of the sixty-one members became infected with COVID-19 and two died.

Justice Kavanaugh then addressed the state's second rationale: that Nevada wants to "jump-start business activity and preserve the economic well-being of its citizens." As he notes, "no precedent suggests that a State may discriminate against religion simply because a religious organization does not generate the economic benefits that a restaurant, bar, casino, or gym might provide. Nevada's rules reflect an implicit judgment that for-profit assemblies are important and religious gatherings are less so; that moneymaking is more important than faith during a pandemic."

This is a great concern. Setting aside the enormous economic benefits society receives from religious organizations, if governments are allowed to discriminate against religious groups on the basis of their perceived economic contributions or lack thereof, we have crossed a red line of grave significance.

Washington Post columnist Henry Olsen stated: "The Bill of Rights exists to protect minorities from the tyrannical exercise of power by majorities. It doesn't matter if the majority subjectively believes it's right or if there is a colorable claim it can appeal to. Religious minorities are minorities, too, and the free-exercise clause is supposed to protect them from tyranny by the mob even when that mob is acting through elected representatives."

Wheaton College dean Ed Stetzer has been a strong advocate for the principle that religious liberty is not violated when churches are asked to submit to governmental regulations, so long as the same regulations apply equally to similar organizations. However, he believes Nevada crossed this line and restricted public worship in ways that were not being applied to similar gatherings, such as in casinos. As a result, he wrote: "For those churches that gather Sunday, contrary to the Nevada governor's order, but by following all the rules that theaters and casinos do, and working to keep their parishioners safe—I stand with you." He explained: "You don't have to agree that churches should be meeting. You don't have to agree that it is safe. However, we can and should agree that churches should not be treated differently than similar contexts. That's fundamental to our approach to religious liberty and in general. This crosses an important line. It's time to speak and time to act."

My position

Here's my position: governmental authorities must not privilege secular gatherings over religious services on the basis of the perceived economic benefits of the former versus the latter. Nor should they apply attendance caps to churches that are not applied to similar gatherings. However, as we have noted, some medical professionals believe that worship services involve activities such as singing and preaching that are known to spread the SARS-CoV-2 virus in ways not found in other public gatherings. People in casinos, restaurants, bars, and gyms do not typically preach or sing.

This factor should be considered as we judge the religious liberty issues related to the Supreme Court's recent rulings on public worship. However, as is customary for such rulings, the five-justice majority did not state their reasoning in either case. Justice Kavanaugh stated that Nevada did not provide "sufficient justification for the differential treatment of religion." I must therefore assume that issues relative to virus transmission through singing and preaching did not play a role in Nevada's case or the majority's decision. If this is true, we should be concerned that the majority's rulings in both cases appear, as the dissenting justices allege, to discriminate against churches and violate their religious freedom.

WEARING MASKS IN PUBLIC

Lily Damtew decided to close her coffee shop after she asked a customer to wear a mask and he spat at her feet and hurled chicken and rice at her window. The neighborhood's support changed her mind. When she reopened six days later, her first customer said, "I see you're open. That takes a lot of courage." You would not think courage would be required to ask customers to wear masks in a pandemic. But that's what was required.

A Family Dollar security guard in Flint, Michigan, was shot and killed after telling a customer that her child had to wear a face mask to enter the store. A Starbucks worker was denounced on social media by a customer who refused to wear a mask. Fights over wearing masks in stores and other public places became so widespread that the *New York Times* called them "the new American pastime."

I have written in the past on the scientific and medical reasons why wearing masks is so important during the pandemic. I understand that some people simply disagree on the merits. They are not convinced by the science I referenced, or they are convinced by those who claim contrary evidence. Of course, the vast majority of those who disagree with mask mandates would never spit at a coffee shop owner or murder a security guard. Nonetheless, this issue became emotional and divisive on a level that transcended the physical act of wearing a facemask.

One skeptic stated, "There's really nothing you can do to hide from the virus." He sees mask mandates in his state as an example of "government over-reach" and adds, "There are people in power who want to see what people will submit to."

The question of wearing masks in public can be especially relevant for public worship since it is difficult to sing or preach and impossible to take communion while wearing one. Several states and communities exempted religious officiants and worship participants from mask-wearing mandates. A large church in Oklahoma encouraged worship attenders to wear masks but did not require them. "I think people would be really discouraged by even stricter, more draconian measures over our First Amendment rights," Executive Pastor Steve Russell explained. One church had an area for those who wanted to wear masks during the service and another for those who did not.

My position: wearing masks in public is demonstrated by numerous scientific studies to be significantly beneficial for others and for those who wear them, constituting an opportunity to love my neighbor as myself (Matthew 22:39). Such a mandate is not an infringement of our civil liberties any more than other statutes that protect citizens and the community (such as speed limits). Neither are mask-wearing mandates in worship an infringement of religious liberty, even when they place an imposition on some religious practices (such as singing and taking communion), so long as they are applied to other public gatherings without consideration of similar practical consequences.

IS THE UNITED STATES BECOMING CHINA?

Christians in China say the persecutions they are now experiencing are worse than what the church experienced during the height of Mao's Cultural Revolution. China's record on human rights, especially with regard to its minorities, is beyond horrific. The Uighurs, a Muslim minority, have been subjected to forced sterilization and abortion in the form of "demographic genocide." Chinese Christians are being pressured to renounce their faith and to spy on other believers.

It has been reported that Christians who receive social welfare payments from the Chinese government have been ordered to remove crosses and religious symbols from their homes or lose their subsidies. One official posted portraits of Mao Zedong and Xi Jinping in a Christian's home and said, "These are the greatest Gods. If you want to worship somebody, they are the ones." I note these horrific developments because they relate to the US's response to the pandemic and could be relevant to religious and civil liberties as a result.

In an article for the *Boston Globe*, cultural psychologist and author Michele Gelfand writes: "The decentralized, defiant, do-it-your-own-way norms that make our country so entrepreneurial and creative also deepen our danger during the coronavirus crisis. To fight this pandemic, we can't just shift our resources; we have to shift our cultural patterns as well." In her view, our nation's conflicted responses to the pandemic "reflect a broader cultural phenomenon. In a loose culture like the United States's, people are simply not used to tightly coordinating their social action toward a common goal and, compared with other nations, we're more ambivalent about sacrificing our freedom for strict rules that constrain our choices."

Dr. Gelfand cites the US, Italy, and Brazil as examples of "looser culture" which "have weaker rules and are much more permissive." She contrasts them with Singapore, Austria, and China as "tight cultures" which have "many rules and punishments governing social behavior." The latter have "histories of famine, warfare, natural disasters, and, yes, pathogen outbreaks" and have learned the hard way that "tight rules and order save lives."

Cultures that have faced few threats, such as the US, "have the luxury of remaining loose. They understandably prioritize freedom over constraint, and they are highly creative and open, but also more disorganized than their tight counterparts." She notes that the US shifted "from loose to tight" during World War II and believes we need to do so again by "temporarily sacrificing liberty for stricter rules" so we can "limit the damage from this disease."

The question, of course, is this: What does "temporarily sacrificing liberty for stricter rules" mean? And will such sacrifices be temporary?

Philosopher Matthew B. Crawford notes that "emergency powers are seldom relinquished once the emergency has passed." He adds: "Bureaucracies have their own interests, quite apart from the public interest that is their official brief and warrant. They are very much in the business of tending and feeding the narratives that justify their existence. Further, given the way bureaucracies must compete for funding from the legislature, each must make a maximal case for the urgency of its mission, hence the necessity of its expansion." I agree with Crawford when he states: "By all means, let us defer to technocratic competence in times of emergency." But, like him, I am also concerned that such deference does not become our permanent posture with regard to governmental authority.

BAD NEWS AND GOOD NEWS ON RELIGIOUS LIBERTY

In August 2020, activists burned a stack of Bibles in front of the federal courthouse in Portland. A statue of Jesus was beheaded at a Miami church in July 2020. A faculty survey at Harvard University in March 2020 found that:

- 79.7 percent considered themselves "very liberal" or "liberal."

- 18.9 percent said they were "moderate."

- only 1.46 percent called themselves "conservative" or "very conservative."

Unsurprisingly, 67 percent of white evangelical Protestants believed Christianity's influence on American life was decreasing. Two-thirds said their beliefs are in conflict with mainstream American culture. Sixty percent said a major cause of this problem is "negative portrayals of Christianity in pop culture"; 43 percent also claimed that "government policies have limited religion's role in public life."

Are our religious freedoms under attack?

In *Bostock v. Clayton County*, the Supreme Court determined that LGBTQ persons must not face employment discrimination, but the court made no allowance for religious objections. However, as religious liberties legal authority David French notes, Title VII of the Civil Rights Act of 1964 "contains a provision specifically designed to protect the autonomy of religious organizations." In his view, this provision "has a profound impact on the relevant applicant pool and (along with the First Amendment) permits employers to require that applicants agree to the organization's statement of faith."

In addition, French reminds us that "religious employers are completely exempt from nondiscrimination statutes when hiring and firing 'ministerial' employees." And religious schools and similar organizations can apply for exemptions to Title IX policies regarding dorm rooms and sexual conduct when "the application of this subsection would not be consistent with the religious tenets of such organization." In other words, religious schools and organizations after *Bostock* can still be exempt from Title IX restrictions on their religious beliefs regarding sexuality and other moral issues.

And French notes that religious organizations and schools increasingly have a right of equal access to public funds and public facilities. He adds that "the same civil rights act that now protects LGBT Americans also explicitly protects people of faith." Employees cannot be harassed because of their religious beliefs or practices or denied a reasonable accommodation of their beliefs or practices.

He adds more good news: "In the face of progressive control of the vast majority of the legal educational establishment, conservatives have created, sustained, and nurtured an intellectually vibrant and determined community of lawyers, scholars, and judges who have transformed American law to better match the meaning and text of the American Constitution. It has not accomplished all it could (what movement ever does?)—and there have been bitter disappointments—but it has made an enormous impact by securing liberties that American Christians now take for granted."

He concludes: "I've spent the vast bulk of my professional life standing guard on the citadel of free exercise and free speech, working to expand its walls and hardening its fortifications. But that citadel exists for a purpose beyond its mere continued existence. It is supposed to empower the church to fearlessly act as salt and light in a broken world."

BIBLICAL RESPONSES TO RELIGIOUS LIBERTY ISSUES

In Chapter 7 of my book, *The State of Our Nation: 7 Critical Issues,* I discuss religious liberty in the context of recent bias against Christians and the challenge of same-sex marriage.

There I note that Christians must resist the temptation to withdraw from culture, choosing instead to take Christ to all nations as fervently and effectively as possible (Matthew 28:19).

Old Testament prophets clearly and consistently spoke out against the cultural sins of their day.

- Hosea condemned the "swearing, lying, murder, stealing, and committing adultery" of his culture (Hosea 4:2). He also warned his society against drunkenness and sexual immorality (4:18) as well.

- Amos condemned enslavement (Amos 1:6–8), mistreatment of pregnant women (1:13) and the poor (2:6), sexual abuse (2:7), drunkenness (4:1), greed (5:11), and corruption (5:12).

- Obadiah warned against violence (v. 10).

- Micah condemned theft (Micah 2:1–2).

Much like the prophets of old, Paul was grieved by idolatry (Acts 17:16) and the sins of his day, many of which he listed specifically (Romans 1:18–32; Galatians 5:19–21). He had "great sorrow and unceasing anguish in [his] heart" (Romans 9:2) for his fellow Jews who had not made Jesus their Messiah. And he gave his life as a missionary to the Gentile world (Galatians 2:7–8).

In his cultural engagement, the apostle followed the example and ministry of our Lord. Jesus fed the hungry (John 6:1–14), healed the sick (Mark 1:33–34), and befriended the outcast (Luke 19:1–10). He taught us to do the same, calling us to be "salt" and "light" (Matthew 5:13–16). Both transform all they contact. As a result, the first Christians gave their goods to anyone who "had need"

(Acts 2:45) and ministered to "the sick and those afflicted with unclean spirits" (Acts 5:16).

Clearly, they did more than "preach the gospel." Or, better said, they preached the gospel of God's love in actions as well as in words. They met felt need in order to meet spiritual need, earning the right to share the message of salvation in Christ.

What do we do when this spiritual calling conflicts with the secular authorities?

SERVING CHRIST AND CAESAR

It was Tuesday of Holy Week. Jesus was teaching the crowds gathered in the Temple corridors. Here, the unlikeliest of political coalitions came against him. The Pharisees hated the Roman occupation, but they also hated Jesus. They considered his grace-centered message to violate the Law and its demands. In their minds, he was a heretic whose influence must be stopped.

The Herodians supported the Roman occupation in every way. They and the Pharisees were in constant political conflict. But they also saw Jesus as a threat to the Empire's power. Like the Pharisees, they wanted him arrested or even killed. So, they "went out and plotted how to entangle him in his words" (Matthew 22:15). Luke gives us their underlying motive: "They hoped to catch Jesus in something he said, so that they might hand him over to the power and authority of the governor" (Luke 20:20 NIV).

The Pharisees sent some of their "disciples" to him (Matthew 22:16), students at one of the two Pharisaic theological seminaries in Jerusalem. Their youth might endear them to Jesus; at any event, they would be less recognizable to him than their leaders. After patronizing him with compliments, they asked their entrapping question: "Is it lawful to pay taxes to Caesar, or not?" (v. 17). Their grammar required a yes or no answer. And either would serve their purpose.

They pushed a very hot button. The "taxes" to which they referred were the poll-tax or "census" tax paid by all males over the age of fourteen and all females over the age of twelve. It was paid directly to the Emperor himself. And it required the use of a coin despised by the Jewish populace. This was the "denarius," a silver coin minted by the Emperor himself. It was the only Roman coin that claimed divine status for the Caesar. On one side, it pictured the head of Emperor Tiberius with the Latin inscription, "Tiberius Caesar son of the divine Augustus." On the other side, it pictured Pax, the Roman goddess of peace, with the Latin inscription "high priest." It was idolatrous in the extreme.

The tax it paid led to a Jewish revolt in AD 6, which established the Zealot movement. That movement eventually resulted in the destruction of Jerusalem and the Jewish nation in AD 70. At this time, that movement was growing in power and influence.

Thus, these schemers were asking Jesus to take a position on the most inflammatory issue of the day. If he said that it is right to pay taxes to Caesar, the public would turn from him in revolt and his influence would be at an end. If he said that it is *not* right to pay taxes to Caesar, Jesus would be a traitor to Rome, and the authorities would arrest and execute him. Either way, the hands of his opponents would be clean, and they would be rid of their enemy.

Here is Jesus' timeless answer: He asked for a denarius, and then he asked them, "Whose likeness and inscription is this?" (v. 20). They told him that it bore the image and inscription of Caesar. And he replied, "Render to Caesar the things that are Caesar's, and to God the things that are God's" (v. 21).

If taxes belong to the nation, pay them. If worship belongs to God, give it. Give to each what is due. Live in two countries, a citizen of both.

Ambassadors for Christ

Paul clarifies this image of citizenship when he called us "ambassadors for Christ" (2 Corinthians 5:20). An American ambassador lives in a foreign country under appointment by his president at home. They obey the laws of that nation. They give allegiance to its leaders and people. But they always have a second allegiance, an even higher allegiance to their home country and their leader. And if they must choose between the two, their loyalties are clear.

Like secular ambassadors, we are each to obey and support our governing authorities:

- "Let every person be subject to the governing authorities. For there is no authority except from God, and those that exist have been instituted by God" (Romans 13:1).

- "This is also why you pay taxes, for the authorities are God's servants, who give their full time to governing. Give everyone what you owe them: If you owe taxes, pay taxes; if revenue, then revenue; if respect, then respect; if honor, then honor" (Romans 13:6–7 NIV).

- "I urge that supplications, prayers, intercessions, and thanksgivings be made for all people, for kings and all who are in high positions, that we may lead a peaceful and quiet life, godly and dignified in every way" (1 Timothy 2:1–2; cf. Titus 3:1–2).

But we are also to obey and serve our Lord:

- "The fear of the Lord is the beginning of knowledge; fools despise wisdom and instruction" (Proverbs 1:7).

- "O kings, be wise; be warned, O rulers of the earth. Serve the Lord with fear, and rejoice with trembling. Kiss the Son, lest he be angry, and you perish in the way, for is wrath is quickly kindled. Blessed are all who take refuge in him" (Psalm 2:10–12).

- "By me kings reign and rulers decree what is just; by me princes rule, and nobles, all who govern justly" (Proverbs 8:15–16).

This balance between reverence for Christ and respect for Caesar is captured in Peter's admonition: "Be subject for the Lord's sake to every human institution, whether it be to the emperor as supreme, or to governors as sent by him to punish those who do evil and to praise those who do good. . . . Honor everyone. Love the brotherhood. Fear God. Honor the emperor" (1 Peter 2:13–14, 17).

Note that we are to "honor" the emperor, but we are to "fear" only God. This means that if we must choose, we must choose our highest authority. We should come to this position only if we must, first seeking every means to obey the secular authorities while remaining true to our Lord. But there are times when we must declare with the apostles, "We must obey God rather than men" (Acts 5:29).

We are to love people, fear God, and honor the state.

We are not to fear people or the state but God alone. In other words, serve your highest authority. When you can serve Christ and state, serve both. If you must choose, choose Christ.

In 2017, Chinese officials began ordering Christians to replace images of Jesus in their homes with posters of President Xi Jinping. I know believers in Cuba who have been told that they would have better jobs for themselves and schools for their children if they would renounce their commitment to Christ.

Even when we must oppose political leaders, we must do so in the character of Christ. It is imperative that we seek the empowering of the Spirit (Ephesians 5:18) in order to manifest the "fruit of the Spirit" (Galatians 5:22–23). We are to be respectful (Titus 3:2), considerate (1 Timothy 2:2), and reverent (1 Peter 3:15).

We need to go to those with whom we disagree, speaking *to* them rather than *about* them (cf. Matthew 18:15).

And we must never say *about* them what we would not say *to* them. We must refuse slander (cf. Psalm 101:5) and deceit (Exodus 20:16), "speaking the truth in love" always (Ephesians 4:15). It is urgent to remember that we represent the Lord in all we say and do.

But we are also to be bold (Acts 4:29; Ephesians 6:19), strong (1 Corinthians 16:13), and courageous (Philippians 1:28) in serving our Lord. When the Sanhedrin demanded that the apostles stop preaching the gospel, "Peter and the other apostles answered, 'We must obey God rather than men'" (Acts 5:29).

Serve your highest authority, always.

CONCLUSION

As David French noted, religious liberty is "supposed to empower the church to fearlessly act as salt and light in a broken world." He is right: religious freedom is a means to the end of spiritual freedom. American Christians can have complete liberty to preach the gospel and seek to win others to Christ, but if we do not preach the gospel and seek to win others to Christ, such liberty loses its eternal significance.

I am grateful for the advances with regard to religious liberty that David French discusses. However, I am concerned about the temptation to trust secular authorities to protect us from secular abuses. Court compositions can change quickly, and justices do not always rule in ways that are consistent with their previous decisions or perceived beliefs. In other words, the church must seize the opportunity that is ours today, using our religious freedom to share spiritual freedom in Christ as fully and effectively as possible.

I have been privileged to teach doctoral seminars for Dallas Baptist University at Oxford University several times over the years. We always make it a point to visit the Martyr's Memorial. It commemorates three Protestant martyrs: Thomas Cranmer, Nicholas Ridley, and Hugh Latimer. The three were burned at the stake near this location: Latimer and Ridley in 1555, and Cranmer the next year.

As the flames rose around Latimer and Ridley, Latimer said to his fellow martyr, "Be of good comfort, Mr. Ridley, and play the man! We shall this day light such a candle by God's grace, in England, as I trust never shall be put out." I have taught the word of God at this very location. The candle they lit "never shall be put out." We are called to shine it in our dark culture with grace and courage, to the glory of God.

A DISCUSSION GUIDE ON RELIGIOUS LIBERTY

The following discussion guide may be used in a small group setting or for your personal time of devotion. We hope it helps you both better understand the topic and how God might want to use you, in your specific context, to be "salt and light" on this issue. A PDF download is available at denisonforum.org/courage-questions.

1. Read Acts 5:17–33. Then consider the questions posed in this chapter's introduction:

    •   Are America's Christians facing threats to our religious liberty on such a level that we must stand up at any cost? Have we reached that point where we must say to secular authorities, "We must obey God rather than men" (Acts 5:29)?

    •   If you agree, name a few examples of recent threats to our religious liberty.

    •   If you disagree, discuss why American Christians have not reached that point. Consider comparing our current cultural and governmental climate to that of the early Christians.

2. Two Supreme Court cases, spurred by church closures in light of the coronavirus pandemic, are cause for concern. In each case, a 5–4 ruling went against a church's request to reopen. In each case, the dissenting opinions noted how the final ruling "indisputably discriminates against religion, and such discrimination violated the First Amendment."

- First, take the side of the majority opinion. Why do you think they voted as they did? (Read the major opinion of *South Bay United Pentecostal Church v. Newsom.*)

- Next, take the side of the dissenting opinion. Why did they dissent?

- Why are these narrow rulings cause for concern for Christians?

3. Is the US becoming like China with regard to a lack of religious liberty?

- Why might people think we are becoming like China? Why might people think such fears are an overreaction? Use examples from the larger culture and your more immediate circles to support your answer.

- Do you believe that any governmental restrictions put in place as a response to current events will be relinquished once the pandemic is over? Why or why not?

4. Do you believe that Christianity's influence on America is increasing or decreasing?

- How would you argue your position?

5. In your personal life, do you tend to withdraw, withstand, or go forth into the culture? In other words, when pressed to take a stand on a sensitive cultural issue (e.g., abortion, same-sex marriage), do you retreat or stay silent? Do you answer only when asked? Are you proactive? Or even aggressive?

- What are some of the benefits associated with each approach? What are some of the dangers?

- How do you navigate the fine line of "speaking the truth in love" (Ephesians 4:15)? What are some ways you can do that through both words and actions?

6. Read Matthew 22:15–22.

   - Why was Jesus' answer to the Pharisees such that "they marveled" after having heard it?

   - How is "Render to Caesar's the things that are Caesar's, and to God the things that are God's" relevant to your life today?

7. How can you be an "ambassador for Christ" in the following areas (2 Corinthians 5:20)?

   - In your home?

   - At your job?

   - In your neighborhood?

   - With your friends and family?

   - At your church?

   - Online?

   - In the world at large?

CHAPTER 5

THE POWER OF HISTORY:
What does the Bible say about removing statues?

Frederick Douglass was one of America's greatest orators, abolitionists, social reformers, and statesmen. After escaping from slavery in Maryland, he became a national leader of the abolitionist movement. On July 5, 1852, he delivered the address, "What to the Slave is the Fourth of July?" A statue of Douglass was eventually erected in Rochester, New York, where he lived and worked for twenty-five years. On the 168th anniversary of his most famous speech, the statue was torn from its base and damaged.

STATUARY, SAINTS, AND PRESIDENTS

On July 4, 2020, Newton Falls, Ohio, declared itself a "Statuary Sanctuary City." Its proclamation welcomed statues rejected by other cities across the United States. It may not have enough room for them all. At this writing, a

Wikipedia article listed 154 statues or monuments in the US that have been toppled, removed, or scheduled for removal. Among them was a statue of Hans Christian Heg, a Union Army colonel in the Civil War and an abolitionist. A bust of Ulysses S. Grant, who led the Union Army to victory, was toppled by protesters.

The Wikipedia article lists twenty-nine statues or busts of Christopher Columbus that have been decapitated, toppled, or removed. On July 4, 2020, protesters pulled down one such statue in Baltimore and threw it into the city's Inner Harbor. A petition in Cleveland, Ohio, proposed replacing a statue of Columbus in its Little Italy neighborhood with a statue to Chef Boyardee, the Italian chef mascot behind the canned goods company.

On July 7, 2020, four Confederate statues in Richmond, Virginia, were removed. Statues of Stonewall Jackson, Matthew Fontaine Maury, and J. E. B. Stuart were taken down by the city; a statue of Jefferson Davis was torn down by protesters.

On July 1, 2020, the city of Columbus, Ohio, named for the Italian navigator, removed a statue of Columbus from in front of its City Hall. The decision was hailed by those who say Columbus statues honor the explorer's genocidal cleansing of the New World and exploitation of Native people. It was opposed by Italian-Americans who say the statues are works of art that forge goodwill and should be preserved.

According to Wikipedia, six statues of Junipero Serra have been toppled or removed. The eighteenth-century Spanish Franciscan friar founded missions across Mexico before arriving in San Diego in 1769 and founding a mission there. According to San Francisco Archbishop

Salvatore Cordileone, "St. Serra made historic sacrifices to protect the indigenous people of California from their Spanish conquerors, especially the soldiers. . . . He walked all the way to Mexico City to obtain special faculties of governance from the Viceroy of Spain in order to discipline the military who were abusing the Indians. And then he walked back to California." Serra was canonized as a saint by Pope Francis during a trip to the US in 2015.

However, statues of St. Serra were attacked on the claim that "Native Americans brought into the mission to be evangelized were not allowed to leave the grounds. Many labored for no pay. There is evidence of beatings, imprisonment and other abuse at the hands of the missionaries." His defenders, however, say that he frequently pleaded for more merciful treatment for the Native Americans under their control. In their view, it is unfair to judge him by twenty-first-century standards.

Lucian K. Truscott IV wrote a *New York Times* article titled "I'm a Direct Descendant of Thomas Jefferson. Take Down His Memorial." He states that the memorial "is a shrine to a man who during his lifetime owned more than 600 slaves and had at least six children with one of them, Sally Hemings."

Stone Mountain, the world's largest Confederate monument, has come under special scrutiny. The carving of Robert E. Lee, Stonewall Jackson, and Jefferson Davis is enormous—Lee is the size of a nine-story building; an adult could stand up inside the mouth of one of the horses. The mountain into which the monument was carved hosted the rebirth of the Ku Klux Klan in 1915, as well as the Klan's first recorded cross burning. Some have proposed blasting the carving from the mountain, filling it in with similar-colored concrete, adding elements such as a bell tower dedicated to Dr. Martin Luther King Jr., or halting the cleaning of the carving.

The controversy over the Emancipation Memorial at Lincoln Park in Washington, DC, is especially complicated. Eleven years after President Lincoln was assassinated, this statue was unveiled to honor him. It depicts him standing and holding a copy of the Emancipation Proclamation as an unshackled black man in a loincloth kneels at his feet. Much of the money for the project was donated by freed slaves, which is why it is known as the Freedmen's Memorial. Former congressman Jesse Jackson Jr. (D-Ill.) argued that the statue should stay: "It's not just a statue of a man being subservient to Lincoln. We can't tear down everything. You can't on the one hand, celebrate Juneteenth . . . and then tear down the statue that marks the event. How much sense does that make?"

Others note that while the $20,000 needed for construction was provided by freed black people, the committee that decided how the statue would look was exclusively white. One critic sees the Black person depicted as "the very archetype of slavery: he is stripped, literally and figuratively, bereft of personal agency, social position, and accoutrements of culture." A defender of the statue countered that the figure is "not kneeling on two knees. He's rising. You look at his hands. . . . He's pushing off. He's not shackled to anyone. He's holding the broken chains of slavery in his hands."

Frederick Douglass spoke at the 1876 unveiling ceremony. According to one of his biographers, "No African American had ever faced this kind of captive audience, of all the leadership of the federal government in one place; and no such speaker would ever again until Barack Obama was inaugurated president in January 2009."

ARGUMENTS FOR AND AGAINST REMOVING STATUES

A June 2020 poll found that 45 percent of Americans see statues of Confederate war heroes as symbols of Southern pride, while 36 percent view them as symbols of racism. Forty-five percent believe they should not be removed from public property, while 38 percent feel they should be removed. However, 60 percent believe that statues of American presidents who were slaveholders should not be removed. The survey demonstrates the complexity of this divisive and emotional issue. Approaches can be grouped into three categories.

Arguments defending statues

One: Historical figures should be judged by their times, not by ours.

Jonah Goldberg believes that the morality of historical figures and events should be judged "not for what came afterwards, but by what came before."

South Dakota Gov. Kristi Noem (R) stated: "We are watching an organized, coordinated campaign to remove and eliminate all references to our nation's founding and many other points in our history. This approach focuses exclusively on our forefathers' flaws, but it fails to capitalize on the opportunity to learn from their virtues." She added, "Make no mistake, this is being done deliberately to discredit America's founding principles by discrediting the individuals who formed them so that America can be remade into a different political image."

British Prime Minister Boris Johnson similarly responded to threats against the statue of Winston Churchill in

Parliament Square, calling the statue "a permanent reminder of his achievement in saving this country—and the whole of Europe—from a fascist and racist tyranny." Johnson noted that Churchill "sometimes expressed opinions that were and are unacceptable to us today, but he was a hero, and he fully deserves his memorial." He added: "We cannot now try to edit or censor our past. We cannot pretend to have a different history. The statues in our cities and towns were put up by previous generations." He notes that earlier generations had different perspectives and claims that to tear the statues down would be to "lie about our history."

Two: We should preserve controversial statues in order to learn from them.

African American and former Secretary of State Condoleezza Rice disagrees with tearing down statues honoring slave owners: "When you start wiping out your history, sanitizing your history to make you feel better, it's a bad thing." Her position: "I'm a firm believer in 'keep your history before you.' And so I don't actually want to rename things that were named for slave owners. I want us to have to look at the names and recognize what they did, and be able to tell our kids what they did and for them to have a sense of their own history."

Georgia Gov. Brian Kemp signed a bill last year protecting his state's Confederate monuments, stating: "It is true that there are monuments in our history that do not reflect our values. We cannot erase them from our history. We must learn from them. These monuments and markers remind us of how far we've come not only as a state but as a country."

Catesby Leigh, a commentator on public art and architecture, writes that many monuments that implicitly enshrine the Confederate "Lost Cause" to vindicate state's rights ignored the issue of slavery. In his view, "these statues . . . still retain cultural value as part of the historic fabric of American communities. More specifically, most Americans can appreciate that such monuments retain artistic value apart from any ideological baggage they might carry simply because they are of higher quality than the memorials we are apt to produce today."

Catholic Archbishop Timothy Dolan notes that even the Bible is full of flawed characters. In his view, the destruction of monuments only impoverishes our sense of history: "As a historian by training, I want to remember the good and the bad, and recall with gratitude how even people who have an undeniable dark side can let light prevail and leave the world better. I want to keep bringing classes of schoolchildren to view such monuments, and to explain to them how even such giants in our history had crimes, unjust acts, and plain poor judgment mixed in with the good we honor."

Three: We should resist anarchy and violations of the rule of law.

President Trump signed an executive order in June 2020 that called on the US government to prosecute individuals who damage statues or monuments. The order also limited federal support to states and law-enforcement agencies that do not protect them.

Security expert Cully Stimson describes five different DC laws that are broken when statues are disfigured or removed apart from the legal process:

- Malicious burning, destruction, or injury of another's property

- Assault on members of police forces, campus or university special police, or fire departments

- Throwing stones or other missiles

- Disorderly conduct

- Disorderly conduct in public buildings or grounds; injury to or destruction of United States property

Writing in the *Federalist*, Emily Jashinsky claims that those who are destroying statues are "blowing up American culture because that is the logical conclusion of an ideology that trains adherents to see every institution as soaked in white supremacy. Scorched cultural earth is their only meaningful tool of reform."

Arguments for adding statues

Frederick Douglass wrote a letter to the *National Republican* newspaper regarding the Emancipation Memorial:

> Sir: Admirable as is the monument by Mr. Ball in Lincoln park, it does not, as it seems to me, tell the whole truth, and perhaps no one monument could be made to tell the whole truth of any subject which it might be designed to illustrate. The mere act of breaking the negro's chains was the act of Abraham Lincoln and is beautifully expressed in this monument. But the act by which the negro was made a citizen of the United States was preeminently the act of President U. S. Grant, and this is nowhere seen in the Lincoln monument. The negro here, though rising, is still on his knees and nude. What

> I want to see before I die is a monument
> representing the negro, not couchant on his
> knees like a four-footed animal, but erect on
> his feet like a man. There is room in Lincoln
> park for another monument, and I throw out
> this suggestion to the end that it may be taken
> up and acted upon.

African American writer Kira Davis states: "Our story is intricately and intimately connected to the 'original sin' of our nation's founding. Not only that, our development has been through Western progression. Western history is black history. Black history is American history. We'll be erasing our own history if we allow the mobs to erase what currently stands." Rather, she wants to "acknowledge the glorious story of a race of captives who built a superpower with blood and sweat and deep grief and still went on to become one of the most influential cultures on the planet." As a result, she states, "Perhaps we should not be seeking to obliterate problematic monuments from our culture. Maybe instead we should consider leaving them be, and then building new monuments, new statues, new symbols alongside them. Instead of reshaping history, let's build it out and up. Let's add the layers that are finally being recognized. Destruction without resurrection is simply empty chaos."

Arguments for removing statues

One: Slaveholders must not be honored.

New York Times columnist Charles Blow is unequivocal: "Slave owners should not be honored with monuments in public spaces. We have museums for that, which also provide better context. This is not an erasure of history, but rather a better appreciation of the horrible truth of it."

Blow states, "On the issue of American slavery, I am an absolutist: enslavers were amoral monsters." He describes the horrors of slave trafficking and the unspeakable suffering Africans endured while being shipped across the Atlantic. He notes that while some say enslavers were people of their time, other men and women of their time found slavery morally reprehensible. He also notes the claim that some enslavers were kinder than others but replies that "the withholding of another person's freedom is itself violent." He states that George Washington enslaved more than one hundred human beings, authorized slavers to stalk runaways even in free states, and pursued one of his escaped slaves "relentlessly, sometimes illegally." He concludes, "No person's honorifics can erase the horror he or she has inflicted on others."

Two: Confederate memorials must be removed.

President Joe Biden believes that Confederate monuments belong in museums rather than public squares but says it is best to remove them peacefully and lawfully.

Philosopher Thomas R. Wells claims that allowing such monuments to stand emboldens white supremacists today: "Erecting statues in honor of white supremacists—not to mention renaming streets and schools after them and flying their flag from state buildings—creates an environment saturated with signals about their political strength and the political weakness of the oppressed. In such an environment the supporters of continued domination can feel confident expressing their views and acting on them without fear of ever being held answerable. Even though they may be an absolute minority of the population they are secure in their position as the *political* winners" (his emphasis).

Architect and college professor James C. McCrery II claims that mobs destroying Confederate statues are doing what governments should have done long ago. He believes that "the great population of statues being destroyed in protest now were themselves erected in a form of protest: Defiance of Union victory, defiance of the emancipation of slaves, defiance of the resulting economic shifts, and defiance of being made to live out the fact that all men are created equal." He states that the South "founded and named parks, libraries, schools, and colleges for their defeated heroes. . . . They hired the best artists and spent lavish amounts of then-rare cash to erect magnificent statuary to their heroes." He disagrees strongly with mobs that are destroying them in violation of civility and legality but believes that "these statues to the defiant South's heroes should have been removed as responsible acts of rational state legislatures."

Poet Caroline Randall Williams describes her body as a "Confederate monument," noting that "the black people I come from were owned and raped by the white people I come from." She writes: "The dream version of the Old South never existed. Any manufactured monument to that time in that place tells half a truth at best. The ideas and ideals it purports to honor are not real." As a result, she says, "the monuments of stone and metal, the monuments of cloth and wood, all the man-made monuments, must come down. I defy any sentimental Southerner to defend our ancestors to me. I am quite literally made of the reasons to strip them of their laurels."

Three: Offensive statues should be replaced.

Historian Sidney Blumenthal and Princeton professor Sean Wilentz have compiled a list of statues they believe should be erected in place of those being removed. Their list includes civil rights leaders, Black soldiers from the Civil War, and African American political leaders. In addition, a statue of former KKK leader and Confederate soldier Nathan Bedford Forrest has stood in the Tennessee Capitol for over forty years but could be replaced by another famous Tennessean. As of 2020, lawmakers in Nashville were considering options to replace Forrest; according to reports, Dolly Parton was one candidate.

THREE CATEGORIES

Russell Moore is an evangelical theologian and ethicist who serves as president of the Ethics & Religious Liberty Commission of the Southern Baptist Convention, the nation's largest Protestant denomination. As usual, his insights on this issue are biblical and relevant.

Dr. Moore suggests a threefold approach to the debate over monuments. One marks a historical event for the education of future generations, such as a marker noting where the Battle of Shiloh took place. A second honors people "in spite of their sins and evils, recognizing some other aspect of their character or service." A third honors people "for their sins and evils." Dr. Moore notes: "The first two are legitimate; the third is not."

He illustrates by asking whether it would be appropriate to depict King David in a church's stained glass. If the artwork recognizes David as psalmist, giant-slayer, obedient king, and member of the throne line that led to Jesus, of course it would. If, however, it eulogizes David leering at Bathsheba or arranging the murder of Uriah, it would be wrong. Dr. Moore's categorization is most helpful in the current debate.

One: Remember history.

Consider his first category: markers and monuments that remind us of historical events. To remove these because we disagree with what happened at these places would be to remove or change the record of history.

I vividly remember my first visit to the Pearl Harbor memorial in Honolulu. As I stood over the submerged remains of the USS Arizona, I thought of the thousands of brave men who died there and across World War II. In no sense does the memorial glorify Japanese aggression or war itself. Rather, it teaches us what happened in the hope that it will not happen again. If we are to remove every historical marker or memorial to events with which someone disagrees, it would be difficult to have historical markers at all.

Two: Honor what is honorable.

The same logic applies to Dr. Moore's second category. Jesus Christ was the only sinless person who ever lived (Hebrews 4:15; Romans 3:23). A statue memorializing any other figure of history can be interpreted by someone to elevate that person's perceived or real flaws.

Regarding Thomas Jefferson, attorney Randy Baker notes: "I have yet to read where anyone suggests that memorials to Jefferson were erected to honor him as a slaveholder. Truly, is that the way he should be judged as a historical figure? Nay, we honor him for his contributions to the American founding, the inspiring words he penned as the author of the Declaration of Independence, and his service as the third President of the United States."

In June 2020, Catholic officials responded to calls for removing a statue of St. Louis' namesake by pointing to all he did to help the poor and the sick. The Archdiocese of St. Louis stated that King Louis IX is "an example of an imperfect man who strived to live a life modeled after the life of Jesus Christ." It noted that the saint and ruler of France during the thirteenth century opened hospitals and shared his daily meals with beggars. Critics said that Louis IX led a violent Crusade against Muslims in the Middle East. The archdiocese responded that those seeking change should focus on policies that will dismantle racism and create a more equal society rather than seeking to "erase history."

Commentator Jonah Goldberg observed: "When people condemn the Founders for keeping slavery intact in slave states, they tend to ignore the context the Founders were living in. The choice they faced wasn't a Constitution with slavery or a Constitution without it. The choice was a Constitution with slavery—or no Constitution at all." He noted that we try not to judge people of other countries and cultures by our standards and adds, "The past is another country, too."

Three: Dishonor what is dishonorable.

Historian Anton Howes writes: "To the minds of people in the eighteenth and nineteenth centuries, public art had a very clear purpose . . . Rather than teaching history, or even celebrating the memory of a particular person, so much of the art that still dots our public places was explicitly about inculcating virtue—good morals, and good habits." If, over time, we come to believe that statues do not "inculcate the virtues that they were supposed to," they should be removed and replaced with a statue that "inculcates the virtues that we need." In this view, a statue could have been erected for one purpose, such as remembering the Confederate dead or paying tribute to states' rights. Over time, however, it comes to be viewed as glorifying slavery and rebellion. In this case, it should be removed and replaced.

Princeton professor Sean Wilentz takes a different approach. In his view, "There can be no doubt that statues of Davis, Lee, John C. Calhoun and others are tributes to slavery, secession and racial domination. They were built for precisely those reasons. They have no other possible meaning, apart from transparent euphemisms about states' rights and federal tyranny. But the same is not true of the Jefferson Memorial in Washington, D.C., with its paeans to universal enlightenment, equality and religious freedom. It is not true of the Lincoln Memorial, a living monument that for decades has been a touchstone for the nation's freedom struggles." Rather than deciding the merits of statues based on shifting public opinion, he warns: "Unless we can outgrow the conception of history as a simplistic battle between darkness and light—unless we can seek understanding of what those in the past struggled with, as we hope posterity will afford to us—we will be the captives of arrogant self-delusions and false innocence."

How to know the difference

Given that none of us is without sin, how are we to distinguish between memorials that should be affirmed (category two) and those that should be questioned (category three)?

History professor Jeffrey Collins suggests, "A simple test might ask: What was the purpose of this monument? What was it intended to honor? If that purpose is either historically dead and thus safely inoffensive . . . or historically alive and still valued (Churchill), we should avoid devising rationales of condemnation." He notes that the "why" test would doom most statues of Stalin. It might allow Confederate memorials that remember the dead but disallow those celebrating slavery or rebellion. He adds: "Commemorations of Ulysses Grant celebrate him for winning the Civil War, not for waging war on Native Americans. Jefferson is honored for writing the Declaration of Independence, not for holding slaves."

He adds: "Monuments aren't erected in a spirit of blind idolatry. They commemorate particular achievements of imperfect people. There are other mechanisms—schools, documentaries, museums—that instruct us on the flaws of our forebears." However, he states that society today prefers the "me" question over the "why" question: How does this monument offend my community or me? What imperfection of its subject makes me feel unwelcome or unsafe?

He concludes: "If the public space is shaped by an ever-escalating tide of affront, little will survive except passing embodiments of our current sensibilities. A culture of ceaseless contestation would result, a narcissistic society unable to imagine past times—or future ones—that don't accept all of our orthodoxies."

FIVE BIBLICAL PRINCIPLES

The word of God has much to say about statues and this controversy. Consider five biblical principles:

One: Idolatry is sin.

The second commandment is clear: "You shall not make for yourself a carved image, or any likeness of anything that is in heaven above, or that is in the earth beneath, or that is in the water under the earth. You shall not bow down to them or serve them, for I the Lord your God am a jealous God"

(Exodus 20:4–5). This prohibition applied to the golden calf that Aaron constructed and Moses destroyed (Exodus 32). It applied to statues of Baal, the Canaanite deity whose worship would later ensnare the people and threaten their future (cf. 1 Kings 18). It applied as well to Molech, a god worshiped through child sacrifice (Leviticus 18:21).

Idolatry is worshiping or venerating anything or anyone in violation of God's sovereignty and will. We commit idolatry when we honor people and behavior that defies and disobeys his word. In the context of this chapter, venerating racism and slavery are examples of idolatry. Racism is sin. The God who made us all (Genesis 1:27) as descendants from the same parents (Genesis 3:20) loves each of us unconditionally (John 3:16) and sacrificially (Romans 5:8). Since he "shows no partiality" (Acts 10:34), we are all one in Christ Jesus (Galatians 3:28).

Jesus taught that sin is to be confronted, not excused or honored: "If your brother sins against you, go and tell him his fault" (Matthew 18:15). He exposed the hypocrisy of the religious leaders (Matthew 23) and called Simon Peter to repentance (John 21:15–19). To honor racism and its related sins is to dishonor God and his word.

Two: Remembering our history is vital.

When God prepared his people to be freed from Egyptian slavery, he instituted "the Lord's Passover" as a perpetual reminder of their exodus and his love (Exodus 12:11). After the Jews passed through the flooded Jordan River on their way into the Promised Land, the Lord commanded them to "take twelve stones from here out of the midst of the Jordan, from the very place where the priests' feet stood firmly, and bring them over with you and lay them down in the place where you lodge tonight" (Joshua 4:3). For this purpose: "When your children ask in time to come, 'What do these stones mean to you?' then you shall tell them that the waters of the Jordan were cut off before the ark of the covenant of the Lord. When it passed over the Jordan, the waters of the Jordan were cut off. So these stones shall be to the people of Israel a memorial forever" (vv. 6–7).

Their ark contained "a golden urn holding the manna, and Aaron's staff that budded, and the tablets of the covenant" (Hebrews 9:4). The night Jesus was betrayed, he instituted the Lord's Supper and taught us to keep it "in remembrance of me" (1 Corinthians 11:25). These were just some of the physical means by which God's people were to remember our history and his grace. By extension, monuments and memorials constructed for the purpose of marking, remembering, and teaching history are valuable means of preserving our past and preparing our future.

Three: There has been only one perfect person.

As we noted earlier, Jesus is the only perfect person who has ever lived. Even the best of our historical figures had flaws and failures (cf. Romans 3:23).

- Paul the Apostle said of himself, "Formerly I was a blasphemer, persecutor, and insolent opponent" (1 Timothy 1:13) and called himself the "foremost" of sinners" (v. 15).

- Abraham lied about his wife to protect himself (Genesis 20:1–13).

- Moses murdered an Egyptian (Exodus 2:11–12).

- David's sin with Bathsheba was horrific (2 Samuel 11).

- Peter denied Jesus three times (Matthew 26:69–75).

Should statues and artwork depicting them be removed?

Former House Speaker Newt Gingrich writes: "President Franklin Delano Roosevelt worked with segregationists, refused to rescue Jews seeking to flee Germany, and locked up Japanese Americans in camps which later led to the United States paying compensation for such a clear injustice. Should we remove the FDR Memorial on the Mall?"

Columnist Elle Reynolds notes that Margaret Sanger, lauded by Planned Parenthood as a "woman of heroic accomplishments" and a "trailblazer in the fight for reproductive rights," was also a "vocal eugenics activist" who targeted minority populations in her attempts at population control. She also spoke at a Ku Klux Klan rally in 1926. Reynolds also points to reports that Lyndon Johnson was a racist who routinely used the N-word.

In 2019, historian David Greenberg responded to newly revealed FBI records about Dr. Martin Luther King Jr. that make very unfavorable allegations. Greenberg noted:

> Even if the ugliest charges against King are bolstered by additional evidence, that doesn't mean we should talk about renaming Martin Luther King Day, tearing down statues of him, or stripping him of his Nobel Prize. In recent years, we've had altogether too much wrecking-ball history—history that takes public or private flaws or failings as reason to cast extraordinary men and women out of our political or artistic pantheons. Historians know that even the most admirable figures from our past were flawed, mortal beings— bad parents or bad spouses, capable of

violence or cruelty, beholden to sexist or racist ideas, venal or megalomaniac, dishonest or predatory. Awareness of these qualities doesn't mean despising figures once held up as heroes. Rather, it gives us a more complete and nuanced picture of the people who shaped our world.

Four: What inspires some people offends others.

In 1 Corinthians 8, Paul addressed the issue of eating meat offered to idols. Pagan temples of the day offered parts of animals in sacrifice to their gods, then sold this meat in the marketplace or used it in meals and gatherings. The apostle noted that "an idol has no real existence" (v. 4). However, "some, through former association with idols, eat food as really offered to an idol, and their conscience, being weak, is defiled" (v. 7).

Paul knew, by contrast, that "food will not commend us to God. We are no worse off if we do not eat, and no better off if we do" (v. 8). What, then, should be done? "Take care that this right of yours does not somehow become a stumbling block to the weak" (v. 9). He concluded, "If food makes my brother stumble, I will never eat meat, lest I make my brother stumble" (v. 13).

This response would suggest that statues that offend some should be taken down. For example, if some African Americans see Confederate statues as glorifying slavery and racism, we should defer to them and remove these monuments. However, Paul sometimes confronted people without fear that he might offend them. In responding to the Corinthian church's toleration of a man who "has his father's wife" (1 Corinthians 5:1), he demanded that the church "purge the evil person from among you" (v. 13).

When he found Peter deferring to the Judaizers rather than supporting Gentile Christians, he "opposed him to his face, because he stood condemned" (Galatians 2:11). He said of a person who was preaching a false gospel, "let him be accursed" (Galatians 1:9) and asked, "Am I now seeking the approval of man, or of God? Or am I trying to please man?" (v. 10).

In other words, deciding what to do about statues is not as simple as removing them if someone is offended by them. Catholic statues venerating Mary offend some Protestants. Statues of Jesus offend some Muslims. A single person's response could veto an entire community's wishes.

Earlier, I noted with approval Dr. Moore's distinction between monuments intended to honor that which is honorable (category two) and those that were erected to honor that which is dishonorable (category three). Now comes the challenge: knowing which is which. We cited historian Jeffrey Collins' "simple test" that asks, "What was the purpose of this monument?" Here is the problem: Who is to answer his question?

Consider the example of Gen. Robert E. Lee. His father fought with George Washington in the Revolutionary War. Lee graduated second in his class at West Point; Gen. Winfield Scott said of his service during the Mexican-American War that he was "the very best soldier I ever saw in the field." Lee opposed the secession of his native Virginia but refused an invitation to command the Union army, stating he "could take no part in an invasion of the Southern states." He led the Confederate army until surrendering to Gen. Ulysses S. Grant at Appomattox Court House on April 9, 1865. He then became president of Washington College (later Washington and Lee University) in Lexington, Virginia, where he served to his death in 1870.

He wrote to his wife in 1856, "In this enlightened age, there are few I believe, but what will acknowledge, that slavery as an institution, is a moral & political evil in any Country." However, Lee also stated that slavery was "a greater evil to the white man than to the black race." In his view, "The blacks are immeasurably better off here than in Africa, morally, socially & physically. The painful discipline they are undergoing, is necessary for their instruction as a race, & I hope will prepare & lead them to better things. How long their subjugation may be necessary is known & ordered by a wise Merciful Providence. Their emancipation will sooner result from the mild & melting influence of Christianity, than the storms & tempests of fiery Controversy."

He and his wife inherited slaves from her father, who apparently intended that they be freed at his death. In 1862, Lee filed a deed of manumission to free these slaves, individually naming more than 150 of them. Three years earlier, however, when some tried to escape but were caught, one said that Gen. Lee gave orders that they be lashed.

Gen. Lee reportedly did not support rights for black citizens and was largely silent about violence perpetrated by white supremacists during Reconstruction. However, he was also opposed to erecting Confederate monuments, writing in 1869 that it would be wiser "not to keep open the sores of war but to follow the examples of those nations who endeavored to obliterate the marks of civil strife."

All this to say, some see statues of Gen. Lee as tributes to the best of the South. His reputation as a Christian and a defender of states' rights and the "Lost Cause" leads them to see him as an example worthy of honor. Others view him as a leader and example of the Confederate rebellion against our nation and a perpetrator of prejudice and slavery.

Whose opinion should prevail?

Five: We should make communal decisions in community.

Public statues, by definition, affect the public. This chapter is not concerned with private artwork viewed only by a few but with memorials intended to be seen by the communities where it is displayed. As a result, decisions regarding public art should be made by the public.

Scripture teaches, "Let every person be subject to the governing authorities. For there is no authority except from God, and those that exist have been instituted by God" (Romans 13:1). In our context, this principle endorses the rule of law in its local and national expressions. To be specific: when a statue is viewed by some as "category two" (honoring that which is honorable) but others as "category three" (honoring that which is dishonorable), we should decide how to respond by utilizing our governing principles and processes.

Some communities would defer to their elected officials; others would hold elections, petition drives, or referendums; others would find other means of gauging and following the community's wishes. Some communities might remove statues found to be offensive. Others might reframe them by adding other figures (as Frederick Douglass suggested) or installing plaques or other means of educating those who view them. Others might relocate them to museums for this purpose. Still others might replace them with figures considered to be worthier of honor.

After Constantine legalized Christianity in the fourth century, Christians took down idolatrous statues across Athens. During the Reformation, many icons and other devotional images were removed. In today's context, when statues are erected by the public to be viewed by the public, the public should decide how best to respond to questions about their enduring value and significance.

CONCLUSION

The question of removing statues is extremely emotional and divisive. Whatever your position on this issue, you should engage those with whom you disagree with respect: "Do not speak evil against one another, brothers" (James 4:11). We are "to speak evil of no one, to avoid quarreling, to be gentle, and to show perfect courtesy toward all people" (Titus 3:2). We are to "be kind to one another, tenderhearted, forgiving one another, as God in Christ forgave you" (Ephesians 4:32). And we are to seek and speak the truth in love (Ephesians 4:15). We love our neighbor by standing for truth, and we stand for truth by loving our neighbor.

How is the issue of removing statues relevant to you where you live?

How can you respond by loving your neighbor in practical, compassionate ways?

What difference can you make that advances the kingdom of God and the public good?

Dr. Martin Luther King Jr. was right: "Every man must decide whether he will walk in the light of creative altruism or in the darkness of destructive selfishness."

Choose wisely.

A DISCUSSION GUIDE ON REMOVING STATUES

The following discussion guide may be used in a small group setting or for your personal time of devotion. We hope it helps you both better understand the topic and how God might want to use you, in your specific context, to be "salt and light" on this issue. A PDF download is available at denisonforum.org/courage-questions.

1. Of the many examples listed (Frederick Douglass, Hans Christian Heg, Ulysses S. Grant, Christopher Columbus, etc.), do you think any of the statues were justly removed?

2. Refer to Lucian K. Truscott IV's comment that Thomas Jefferson's memorial "is a shrine to a man who during his lifetime owned more than 600 slaves." What is your initial response to this statement?

3. Now consider former congressman Jesse Jackson Jr.'s statement on the statue of Lincoln: "It's not just a statue of a man being subservient to Lincoln. We can't tear down everything. You can't on the one hand, celebrate Juneteenth . . . and then tear down the statue that marks the event. How much sense does that make?" How would you respond to his statement?

4. Why do you think there are so many opinions or differing responses to removing statues?

5. Recall these survey results: "A recent poll found that 45 percent of Americans see statues of Confederate war heroes as symbols of Southern pride, while 36 percent view them as symbols of racism. Forty-five percent believe they should not be removed from public property, while 38 percent feel they should be removed. However, 60 percent believe that statues of American presidents who were slaveholders should not be removed." Do these statistics shock you? Why or why not?

6. Read the following arguments in defense of statues. Do you agree with these reasons? Why or why not? Does one argument strike you as more effective than the others or more important to consider?

   - Historical figures should be judged by their times, not by ours.

   - We should preserve controversial statues in order to learn from them.

   - We should resist anarchy and violations of the rule of law.

   - We should add statues instead of removing ones that already exist.

7. Review the arguments for removing statues. Do you agree with these reasons? Why or why not? Does one argument strike you as particularly more effective than the others or more important to consider?

   - Slaveholders must not be honored.

   - Confederate memorials must be removed.

   - Offensive statues should be replaced.

8. Consider Dr. Moore's threefold approach to the debate over removing statues. What is most important about each step in that approach?

9. Recall: "Idolatry is worshiping or venerating anything or anyone in violation of God's sovereignty and will. We commit idolatry when we honor people and behavior that defies and disobeys his word." And further: "To honor racism and its related sins is to dishonor God and his word." Does this biblical principle change the way you view any of the arguments for and against removing statues? If so, why? Does it change what you believe about removing statues?

10. Recall: "Monuments and memorials constructed for the purpose of marking, remembering, and teaching history are valuable means of preserving our past and preparing our future." How does remembering the past help us prepare for the future? Do you consider it a greater evil to remove a statue that serves as a remembrance or to leave it as a reminder for future generations? Why?

11. Because Jesus was the only perfect person, we can find flaws in every historical figure. How does this point tie into the fact that idolatry is sin? Even as we honor historical figures who acted honorably, how does our honoring of Jesus Christ shape the way we view history and our world?

12. What inspires some people offends others. If some are offended by a statue, we should tear it down, so that they might not stumble. What do you think of this argument? Do you agree with its reasoning?

13. Do you agree with the statement that "decisions regarding public art should be made by the public"? Why or why not?

14. How is the "extremely emotional and divisive" issue of removing statues relevant to you where you live?

15. How can you respond by loving your neighbor in practical, compassionate ways?

16. What difference can you make that advances the kingdom of God and the public good?

17. Finally, has this chapter helped shape your view of the issue? If so, how? Do you feel more equipped to "choose wisely"? Why or why not?

CHAPTER 6

THE LATEST EXPRESSION OF THE POSTMODERN CONTRADICTION:
What does the Bible say about cancel culture?

On July 2, 2020, Niel L. Golightly resigned as Boeing's communications chief because he'd written an article nearly thirty-three years prior that said women should not serve in combat. His article appeared in the December 1987 issue of *Proceedings*, a monthly publication of the US Naval Institute. Golightly was a twenty-nine-year-old Navy pilot when he wrote: "Introducing women into combat would destroy the exclusively male intangibles of war fighting and the feminine images of what men fight for—peace, home, family." He added that, on a five-thousand-man aircraft carrier, "There is simply no room for the problem of sexual harassment, rape, prostitution, pregnancy, love triangles, and adolescent emotional crises."

In an interview, he stated that these views in no way represent what he believes today. Nonetheless, after employee complaints about the 1987 article, he chose to resign for the sake of the company.

CANCELING JIMMY FALLON

"Cancel culture" has been described as "removing of support for public figures in response to their objectionable behavior or opinions. This can include boycotts or refusal to promote their work." For example:

- An editorial page editor at the *New York Times* resigned in the wake of fierce criticism after publishing an opinion piece by the conservative Sen. Tom Cotton.

- A professor at UCLA came under investigation for reading Dr. Martin Luther King Jr.'s "Letter from Birmingham Jail" in his class since it included the N-word.

- Comedian Jimmy Fallon issued a public apology after the hashtag #jimmyfallonisoverparty went viral, protesting a video clip that surfaced from twenty years ago in which he wore blackface to impersonate Chris Rock.

Any of these issues could be addressed through conventional means. By contrast, "cancel culture" approaches use social media to organize an outcry that threatens swift reprisals if its demands are not met immediately. Anyone can organize such a protest, whether their outrage and called-for response are justified or not.

This phenomenon is causing alarm even on the cultural left. *Harper's Magazine* published "A Letter on Justice and Open Debate," which was initially signed by 153 well-known writers and public intellectuals. (Two later withdrew their names.) They warn about "a new set of moral attitudes and political commitments that tend to weaken our norms of open debate and toleration of differences in favor of ideological conformity." In their view, "The free exchange of information and ideas, the lifeblood of a liberal society, is daily becoming more constricted." As a result, "it is now all too common to hear calls for swift and severe retribution in response to perceived transgressions of speech and thought."

Among their examples: "Editors are fired for running controversial pieces; books are withdrawn for alleged inauthenticity; journalists are barred from writing on certain topics; professors are investigated for quoting works of literature in class; a researcher is fired for circulating a peer-reviewed academic study; and the heads of organizations are ousted for what are sometimes just clumsy mistakes." The result, they believe, "has been to steadily narrow the boundaries of what can be said without the threat of reprisal." In their view, "The way to defeat bad ideas is by exposure, argument, and persuasion, not by trying to silence or wish them away."

CANCELING ABRAHAM LINCOLN

Criticism on social media is not "cancel culture" unless it tries to "cancel" its subject in some way. As *New York Times* columnist Ross Douthat writes: "You are not being canceled if you are merely being heckled or insulted . . . no matter how vivid and threatening the heckling becomes. You are decidedly at risk of cancellation, however, if your critics are calling for you to be de-platformed or fired or put out of business."

For example, former Gov. Howard Dean tweeted: "Unfortunately Christians don't have much [of] a reputation for anything but hate these days thanks to Franklin Graham and Jerry Falwell and other trump [sic] friends." His statement, however offensive it might be to Christians, did not then call for a boycott or other actions against us. By contrast, when Goya CEO Robert Unanue made positive statements about President Trump, there were quick calls to boycott his company and its products. (This despite his company's donation of two million pounds of food to food banks during the pandemic and his earlier work with the Obama administration.)

Calls for reprisals against alleged offenses are evident throughout human history. One could say that Saul sought to "cancel" David when he called upon his son and servants to kill his perceived rival (1 Samuel 19:1). In the presidential election of 1800, surrogates of John Adams tried to "cancel" Thomas Jefferson's candidacy by issuing claims against him that make many of today's tweets pale by comparison; surrogates of Jefferson did the same to Adams.

It's inconceivable today, but many newspaper editorials about President Abraham Lincoln and calls for his removal were scathing and vociferous in the Union prior to his assassination. What makes this moment different is that, as Douthat notes, "the heat of the cancel-culture debate reflects the intersection of the internet as a medium for cancellation with the increasing power of left-wing moral norms as a justification for cancellation." He writes: "The emergent, youthful left wants to take current taboos against racism and anti-Semitism and use them as a model for a wider range of limits—with more expansive definitions of what counts as racism and sexism and homophobia, a more sweeping theory of what sorts of speech and behavior threaten 'harm,' and a more precise linguistic etiquette for respectable professionals to follow."

Digital technology makes it possible to call for the cancellation of those who do not adhere to these "moral norms" on an unprecedented level of reach and immediacy. Anyone with access to the internet can post their outrage at perceived offenses. Anyone who "likes" or forwards these posts can join in the instant conflagration. Villanova professor Jill McCorkel adds that this collective canceling of someone creates a sense of community. "It reinforces, at a time of political division, a sense of shared solidarity, at least among the people who are doing the canceling," she said. "It's psychologically intoxicating to feel part of a group and to feel a part of something larger than yourself."

WHAT CHRISTIANS SHOULD EXPECT

Cancel culture is rooted in the postmodern assertion that all truth claims are individual and subjective. Each of us interprets our experiences of the world in ways that are unique to us. As a result, we are told, there can be no such thing as "objective" truth. Conventional wisdom therefore claims that there is only "your truth" and "my truth." (Of course, to deny objective truth is to make an objective truth claim.) Tolerance is therefore the great value of our society. We are told that we must tolerate and affirm any behavior that does not harm others. However, our "tolerant" culture is highly intolerant of anyone it perceives to be intolerant. Cancel culture is just the latest expression of this contradiction.

Supreme Court rulings have protected religious liberty with regard to contraceptives and religious teaching at religious schools. However, these rulings have not addressed the merits of the religious beliefs under such protection. In the minds of many, these rulings have merely protected our "right to discriminate."

Cancel culture picks up where the courts have left off. If you believe that life begins at conception, many will accuse you of waging a "war on women." If you have stated these beliefs publicly, you should not be surprised if abortion advocates surface your statements and use social media to call for reprisals against you and your company, school, church, etc. If you have stated that marriage should be a lifelong covenant between a man and a woman, your "homophobia" and "bigotry" may be used against you. If you have made the biblical statement that Jesus is the only way to heaven, your "intolerance" may likewise lead to reprisals. The more visible your social status and leadership, the more a target you are likely to become.

I often make reference to Richard Niebuhr's classic book, *Christ and Culture*, and his five ways that the two have related historically. His model is useful for this discussion as well.

- A "Christ against culture" approach is to retreat from engagement with the fallen world. We are less likely to be "canceled" if we don't make statements or take stands on social issues. But this approach is difficult to reconcile with our call to be salt and light in our culture (Matthew 5:13–16).

- A "Christ of culture" approach is to adopt the shifting cultural norms of the day. If we change our minds on homosexual activity, for instance, we cannot be accused of homophobia and may be applauded for our tolerance. But the biblical prohibition against such activity is clear, despite claims to the contrary.

- A "Christ above culture" approach is to divorce Sunday from Monday and religion from the "real world." However, to the degree that we are clear about our biblical beliefs, at least with our Christian friends, we risk being criticized for them by secular culture.

- A "Christ and culture in paradox" approach engages cultural issues for the sake of evangelism and ministry but focuses less on cultural transformation. To speak biblical truth on controversial issues, however, is to open ourselves to cancellation, even if we are not attempting to change the culture itself.

- A "Christ transforming culture" approach seeks to change minds, lives, and society. Such initiative will especially face opprobrium and worse.

Jesus was blunt: "If the world hates you, know that it has hated me before it hated you. If you were of the world, the world would love you as its own; but because you are not of the world, but I chose you out of the world, therefore the world hates you" (John 15:18–19). Paul added his warning: "All who desire to live a godly life in Christ Jesus will be persecuted, while evil people and imposters will go on from bad to worse, deceiving and being deceived" (2 Timothy 3:12–13).

Francis Chan noted: "Something is wrong when our lives make sense to unbelievers." As my youth minister used to say, if you and the devil aren't opposing each other, you're probably going in the same direction.

WHAT CHRISTIANS SHOULD DO

How should followers of Christ respond to the "cancel culture" phenomenon?

One: See persecution as a call to courageous perseverance.

David said to the Lord, "Consider how many are my foes, and with what violent hatred they hate me" (Psalm 25:19). This was the experience of someone the Lord described as "a man after my heart" (Acts 13:22). If he faced "violent hatred," we should expect the same. And we should pray for God's protection as we continue to share God's word. Here was the secret to David's courage: "I have set the Lord always before me; because he is at my right hand, I shall not be shaken" (Psalm 16:8). Let's do the same.

Two: Seek the reward of God before the acclaim of the culture.

It is often possible to serve both Christ and Caesar (cf. Matthew 22:21). Joseph was able to serve the Egyptian pharaoh and his Jewish family. Nehemiah was cupbearer to the Persian king and governor of Jerusalem. Esther was queen in Persia as well as her people's protector. But when we must choose, we must choose Christ over Caesar.

Recall what Peter and John said to the Sanhedrin's demand that the apostles cease preaching: "Whether it is right in the sight of God to listen to you rather than to God, you must judge, for we cannot but speak of what we have seen and heard" (Acts 4:19–20). Daniel continued praying to God in defiance of the king's edict (Daniel 6:10). Jeremiah risked his life to speak prophetic truth to the king (cf. Jeremiah 38:14–23).

It is a paradoxical fact that the less we seek the acclaim of people, the more faithfully we can minister to them. Henri Nouwen noted: "We can really be in the world, involved in the world, and actively engaged in the world precisely because we do not belong to it, precisely because that is not where our dwelling place is. Precisely because our home is in God, we can be in the world and speak words of healing, of confrontation, of invitation, and of challenge."

Three: Choose to engage the culture with truth and grace.

Jesus' words are emblazoned on libraries and universities across the land: "You will know the truth, and the truth will set you free" (John 8:32). But context is vital. In the previous verse, our Lord "said to the Jews who had believed in him, 'If you abide in my word, you are truly my disciples'" (v. 31). Only on this condition would they know the truth and be set free by it. Here we learn this vital fact: humans find true freedom only in obedience to the word of God.

As a result, when we speak truth to culture, we are giving others a gift they desperately need but can find nowhere else. Counter to the postmodern claim that all truth is personal and subjective, which makes evangelism and ministry an "imposition" of our beliefs on others, we are sharing good news that is vital and transforming. An oncologist is not intolerant when she tells her patient that he needs lifesaving surgery. An attorney is not intolerant when he advises his client that she needs to plead guilty to avoid an even harsher sentence.

It is urgent that we continue to speak biblical truth to cultural issues. But it is also urgent that we speak the truth "in love" (Ephesians 4:15). In fact, such kindness is especially important as our response to the unkindness of others. Jesus told his followers, "You have heard that it was said, 'An eye for an eye and a tooth for a tooth.' But I say to you, 'Do not resist the one who is evil. But if anyone slaps you on the right cheek, turn to him the other also'" (Matthew 5:38–39). In Jesus' day, the left hand was never used in public. As a result, if I were to slap you "on the right cheek" with my right hand, I must employ a backhanded motion. This is obviously a shaming action rather than a life-threatening attack.

Jesus' words depict physically what "cancel culture," through social media, attempts to do verbally. According to our Lord, we must not respond in kind. Scripture is clear: We are to "put away all malice and all deceit and hypocrisy and envy and all slander" (1 Peter 2:1). Instead, we are "to speak evil of no one, to avoid quarreling, to be gentle, and to show perfect courtesy toward all people" (Titus 3:2). With our words and attitudes, we are to reflect the truth and grace of our Lord.

CONCLUSION

Paul encouraged Timothy to "fight the good fight of the faith" (1 Timothy 6:12). We do this by our personal character: "Pursue righteousness, godliness, faith, love, steadfastness, gentleness" (v. 11). To "pursue" (the Greek word means to "run hard after") these virtues in our fallen culture is indeed a "fight." And we do it by our public words: "Devote yourself to the public reading of Scripture, to exhortation, to teaching" (1 Timothy 4:13). I'm convinced that if Paul were alive today, he would use social media to spread the good news of God's love and the truth of his word. And he would face criticism and worse.

Cardinal Newman was right: "Nothing would be done at all, if a man waited till he could do it so well, that no one could find fault with it." Those who oppose biblical truth may try to cancel those who proclaim it, but we know how the story ends. As my college professor said, we can summarize the book of Revelation in two words: "We win."

In the meantime, let's be faithful to speak biblical truth with biblical grace. Let's remember that those who reject this truth need it the most. And let's choose the courage that honors Jesus and demonstrates the relevance and power of our faith to our fallen world.

Albert Schweitzer testified, "Truth has no special time of its own. Its hour is now—always."

Do you agree?

A DISCUSSION GUIDE ON CANCEL CULTURE

The following discussion guide may be used in a small group setting or for your personal time of devotion. We hope it helps you both better understand the topic and how God might want to use you, in your specific context, to be "salt and light" on this issue. A PDF download is available at denisonforum.org/courage-questions.

1. How do you define cancel culture? How much exposure have you had to cancel culture?

2. Of the three examples of cancel culture presented in the article, which most surprises you? In any of these situations, how would you have responded as the one being canceled? As a spectator?

3. I wrote that "anyone can organize such a protest, whether their outrage and called-for response are justified or not." Why is this a dangerous reality? How can Christians mitigate this effect on social media?

4. What is wrong with the idea of "canceling" someone? For Christians, why is it important to defend freedom of speech?

5. Jill McCorkel says that the collective canceling of someone creates a sense of community. As a Christian, how would you counsel someone who believes that their cancelation of a public figure is for the common good or that participating in a digital boycott gives them a sense of community?

6. I wrote that "cancel culture is rooted in the postmodern assertion that all truth claims are individual and subjective" and that "tolerance is therefore the great value of our society." How has this affected social media? How should we interact with nonbelievers on social media platforms?

7. How should we be mindful of ourselves in our spheres of influence?

8. Refer to the following five ways that Christianity and culture have interacted historically.

   • Christ against culture: retreat from engagement with the fallen world

   • Christ of culture: adopt the shifting cultural norms of the day.

   • Christ above culture: to divorce Sunday from Monday and religion from the "real world."

   • Christ and culture in paradox: engages cultural issues for the sake of evangelism and ministry but focuses less on cultural transformation.

   • Christ transforming culture: seeks to change minds, lives, and society.

Which of the five reflects the way you interact with the world? How about your local community?

9. Reread the passage from John 15:19. Does this alter the way you perceive cancel culture?

10. Consider the three points of response:

   • See persecution as a call to courageous perseverance.

- Seek the reward of God before the acclaim of the culture.

- Choose to engage the culture with truth and grace.

Which of the three sounds most challenging? Which is easier to adopt?

Now consider each point separately. In what ways can you encourage your immediate community to live by each point for the glory of the gospel?

11. How has your perception of cancel culture changed after this study? In what ways are you now more equipped to interact with today's culture?

CHAPTER 7

THE PARDONABLE SIN:
What does the Bible say about suicide?

Darrin Patrick, a megachurch pastor, speaker, and author, died on May 7, 2020. According to Seacoast Church, a multi-site megachurch in South Carolina where he was teaching pastor, he died of what appeared to be a "self-inflicted gunshot wound." A longtime friend of Patrick noted that pastors often don't know what to do when they struggle. They attempt to keep up appearances and handle their struggles on their own. "We don't feel like we can ask for help," he said.

Anxiety is escalating in our culture. According to a 2017 survey, more Americans than ever before were stressed, depressed, and anxiety ridden. Nearly forty million people in the US (18 percent) experience an anxiety disorder in any given year. Anxiety disorders are the most common and pervasive mental disorders in America.

There is a direct link between anxiety and opioid use.

Those suffering from anxiety are two to three times more likely to have an alcohol or other substance abuse disorder. Anxiety is linked to heart disease, chronic respiratory disorders, and gastrointestinal disorders. And numerous studies have related anxiety directly to suicide. Compared to those without anxiety, patients with anxiety disorder were more likely to have suicidal ideations, attempted suicides, completed suicides, or suicidal activities.

These were the facts even before the pandemic that challenged millions of Americans who face mental health issues. According to an August 13, 2020, report by the Centers for Disease Control and Prevention, one in four young adults said they had considered suicide in the previous month because of the COVID-19 pandemic. Roughly 30.9 percent of respondents said they had experienced symptoms of anxiety or depression. A 2020 mental distress survey found that participants were eight times as likely to screen positive for serious mental illness as participants in a similar survey two years ago. The vast majority of the 2020 participants, 70 percent, met the criteria for moderate to serious mental illness. An article in the *New England Journal of Medicine* noted that during public health emergencies, "emotional distress is ubiquitous in affected populations." And counselors warn that the isolation created by stay-at-home restrictions can especially contribute to psychological harm.

As a pastor and a theologian, I am not qualified to offer medical advice or professional counseling to those suffering from anxiety and depression. But I can offer biblical insights on the painful issue of suicide. Let's look at this issue through the lens of Scripture, and let's offer others the hope and help that we find in Christ.

THE SCOPE OF THE ISSUE

The facts of suicide in the US are cause for lament:

- More people die from suicide than from homicide in America.

- According to the Centers for Disease Control and Prevention, suicide rates increased 25 percent nationally from 1999 to 2016. They rose in nearly every state.

- In 2018, according to the Suicide Prevention Resource Center, suicide was the second-leading cause of death for Americans ages ten to thirty-four.

- Suicide rates are much higher in the elderly American population than for any other age group.

- Suicide rates have grown exponentially for women since 1999.

- White, middle-aged men account for 70 percent of all suicides each year.

- The CDC reports that more than half of the people who died by suicide did not have a known mental health condition.

Factors contributing to suicide include:

- relationship problems

- a crisis in the past or upcoming two weeks

- problematic substance abuse

- physical health problems

- job or financial problems

- criminal or legal problems

- loss of housing

These are some of the facts regarding the tragedy of suicide. However, if you are reading this chapter because this subject is more personal than objective for you, I hope the following discussion is helpful. As I noted, I am writing as a theologian and a minister, not a counselor, psychologist, or psychiatrist. I will offer a brief overview of our subject from a biblical and theological perspective, with some practical suggestions at the conclusion. But if suicide is a real issue for you, I urge you to seek professional help immediately. See the section "Help for those considering suicide" toward the end of this chapter.

THE HISTORY OF SUICIDE

The term *suicide* is traced in the *Oxford English Dictionary* to 1651; its first occurrence is apparently in Sir Thomas Browne's *Religio Medici*, written in 1635 and published in 1642. Before it became a common term, expressions such as "self-murder" and "self-killing" were used to describe the act of taking one's own life.

In Greek and Roman antiquity, suicide was accepted and even seen by some as an honorable means of death and the attainment of immediate salvation. Stoics and others influenced by them saw suicide as the triumph of an individual over fate. Socrates' decision to take his own life rather than violate the state's sentence of execution influenced many to see the act as noble. However, he also made clear that we belong to the gods and cannot end our lives unless they wish it so (Plato, *Phaedo* section 62bc).

Many of the early Christians knew they would likely die for their faith but chose to follow Christ at any cost. These deaths are not typically considered "suicide" since they were not initiated by the person but accepted as a consequence of his or her commitment to Jesus.

Augustine (AD 354–430) was a strong opponent of any form of self-murder (cf. *City of God* 1:4–26). He appealed to the sixth commandment and its prohibition against murder. And he agreed with Socrates that our lives belong to God so that we have no right to end them ourselves. Over time, many in the church came to see self-murder as an unpardonable sin. (I discuss the Catholic Church's position later in this chapter.)

In the nineteenth century, social scientists began to view suicide as a social issue and a symptom of a larger dysfunction in the community and/or home. Medical doctors began to identify depression and other disorders behind the act. Suicide became decriminalized so that the individual could be buried, his family not disinherited, and a survivor not prosecuted.

Many are confused about this difficult subject, as our society and its churches have adopted such a wide variety of positions on it. So, let's discuss biblical teachings on the issue, the Catholic position, a Protestant response, and practical help for those dealing with this tragic issue.

THE BIBLE AND SUICIDE

God's word does not use the word *suicide*, but it has much to say on our subject.

Biblical occurrences

The Old Testament records five clear suicides:

1. When Abimelech was mortally wounded by a woman who dropped a millstone on his head, he cried to his armor-bearer to kill him so his death would not be credited to the woman (Judges 9:54).

2. The mortally wounded King Saul fell upon his own sword lest the Philistines abuse him further (1 Samuel 31:4).

3. Saul's armor-bearer then took his own life as well (1 Samuel 31:5).

4. Ahithophel hanged himself after his advice was no longer followed by King David's son Absalom (2 Samuel 17:23).

5. Zimri set himself afire after his rebellion failed (1 Kings 16:18).

Additionally, some consider Jonah to have attempted suicide (Jonah 1:11–15). And Samson destroyed the Philistine temple, killing himself and all those with him (Judges 16:29–30). But many do not see this as a suicide as much as an act of military bravery.

The death of Judas is the only clear example of suicide in the New Testament (Matthew 27:3–10). Paul later prevented the suicide of the Philippian jailer and won him to Christ (Acts 16:27–28). Some consider Jesus' death to have been a kind of suicide since he made clear: "No one takes [my life] from me, but I lay it down of my own accord" (John 10:18). However, as the divine Son of God, he could only have been killed, by any means, with his permission.

Biblical principles

God's word makes clear the sanctity of life:

- "You shall not murder" (Exodus 20:13).

- "I call heaven and earth to witness against you today, that I have set before you life and death, blessing and curse. Therefore choose life, that you and your offspring may live" (Deuteronomy 30:19).

- "The Lord gave and the Lord has taken away; blessed be the name of the Lord" (Job 1:21).

- "Do you not know that your body is a temple of the Holy Spirit within you, whom you have from God? You are not your own, for you were bought with a price. So glorify God in your body" (1 Corinthians 6:19–20).

- "No one ever hated his own flesh, but nourishes and cherishes it, just as Christ does the church" (Ephesians 5:29).

There are times when believers may have to give their lives in the service of Christ and his kingdom (cf. Mark 8:34–36; John 13:37; Philippians 1:21–22). But voluntary martyrdom is not usually considered suicide.

Our postmodern culture claims that absolute truth does not exist (note that this is an absolute truth claim). In a nontheistic or relativistic society, it is difficult to argue for life and against suicide. If we are our own "higher power," we can do with our lives what we want, or so we're told. But if God is the Lord of all that is, he retains ownership over our lives and our days. He is the only one who can determine when our service is done, our intended purpose fulfilled. It is the clear and consistent teaching of Scripture that our lives belong to their Maker and that we are not to end them for our own purposes.

SUICIDE AND THE CATHOLIC CHURCH

Does this fact mean that suicide costs Christians their salvation?

Many of the theological questions people ask in this regard relate in some way to the Catholic Church's teachings on the subject. The Catholic Catechism contains several statements regarding suicide and mortal sin (all italics are in the original).

The Catholic Church on suicide

On suicide, the Church does not maintain that taking one's own life always leads to eternity in hell, as this statement makes clear, from the *Catechism of the Catholic Church*:

> #2280 Everyone is responsible for his life before God who has given it to him. It is God who remains the sovereign Master of life. We are obliged to accept life gratefully and preserve it for his honor and the salvation of our souls. We are stewards, not owners, of the life God has entrusted to us. It is not ours to dispose of.

> #2281 Suicide contradicts the natural inclination of the human being to preserve and perpetuate his life. It is gravely contrary to the just love of self. It likewise offends love of neighbor because it unjustly breaks the ties of solidarity with family, nation, and other human societies to which we continue to have

obligations. Suicide is contrary to love for the living God.

#2282 If suicide is committed with the intention of setting an example, especially to the young, it also takes on the gravity of scandal. Voluntary co-operation in suicide is contrary to the moral law.

Grave psychological disturbances, anguish, or grave fear of hardship, suffering, or torture can diminish the responsibility of the one committing suicide.

#2283 We should not despair of the eternal salvation of persons who have taken their own lives. By ways known to him alone, God can provide the opportunity for salutary repentance. The Church prays for persons who have taken their own lives.

The Catholic Church on mortal sin

The Catholic Church maintains a distinction between "mortal" and "venial" sins. Mortal sins separate us from God's grace; venial sins, while serious, do not. The Catechism states:

> #1037 God predestines no one to go to hell; for this, a willful turning away from God (a mortal sin) is necessary, and persistence in it until the end. In the Eucharistic liturgy and in the daily prayers of her faithful, the Church implores the mercy of God, who does not want "any to perish, but all to come to repentance."

#1859 Mortal sin requires full knowledge and complete consent. It presupposes knowledge of the sinful character of the act, of its opposition to God's law. It also implies a consent sufficiently deliberate to be a personal choice. Feigned ignorance and hardness of heart do not diminish, but rather increase, the voluntary character of a sin.

#1860 Unintentional ignorance can diminish or even remove the imputability of a grave offense. But no one is deemed to be ignorant of the principles of the moral law, which are written in the conscience of every man. The promptings of feelings and passions can also diminish the voluntary and free character of the offense, as can external pressures or pathological disorders. Sin committed through malice, by deliberate choice of evil, is the gravest.

#1861 Mortal sin is a radical possibility of human freedom, as is love itself. It results in the loss of charity and the privation of sanctifying grace, that is, of the state of grace. If it is not redeemed by repentance and God's forgiveness, it causes exclusion from Christ's kingdom and the eternal death of hell, for our freedom has the power to make choices for ever, with no turning back. However, although we can judge that an act is in itself a grave offense, we must entrust judgment of persons to the justice and mercy of God.

#2268 The fifth commandment forbids direct and intentional killing as gravely sinful.

The murderer and those who cooperate voluntarily in murder commit a sin that cries out to heaven for vengeance.

#1470 . . . it is only by the road of conversion that we can enter the Kingdom, from which one is excluded by grave sin. In converting to Christ through penance and faith, the sinner passes from death to life and "does not come into judgment."

Theological principles

The following principles of Catholic theology seem clear:

- We cannot be sure of the spiritual state of the person who commits suicide. This person may be suffering from "grave psychological disturbances" which "can diminish the responsibility of the one committing suicide" (#2282). Mortal sin requires "full knowledge and complete consent" (#1859) and can be diminished by unintentional ignorance (#1860).

- Thus, the Church "should not despair of the eternal salvation of persons who have taken their own lives" (#2283).

- However, if the person was fully aware of his or her actions, without suffering "grave psychological disturbances," this person committed murder, an act that is "gravely sinful" (#2268).

- A person who commits a mortal sin and demonstrates "persistence in it until the end" goes to hell (#1037).

Since a person who commits self-murder (suicide) cannot then repent of this sin, it is logical to conclude that this person cannot be saved from hell. However, the Catechism nowhere makes this conclusion explicit.

IS SUICIDE THE UNPARDONABLE SIN?

Most Protestants do not believe that it is possible for a Christian to lose his or her salvation, even if that person commits suicide. In this section, we'll summarize biblical principles on the subject of "eternal security." Then we'll apply them to the issue of suicide.

Know what you can know

The Bible assures us, "I write these things to you who believe in the name of the Son of God, that you may know that you have eternal life" (1 John 5:13). A literal translation would be, "We can actually and with full assurance know intellectually and personally that we have eternal life." This phrase does not mean that we gradually grow into assurance, but that we can possess here and now a present certainty of the life we have already received in Jesus.

But first we must "believe in the name of the Son of God." "Believe" means more than intellectual assent—it is the biblical word for personal trust and commitment. We can assent to the fact that an airplane will fly me from Dallas to Atlanta, but I must get on board before it can. No surgeon can operate on the basis of intellectual assent—we must submit to the procedure. If you have made Christ your Savior, you can claim the biblical fact that you "have eternal life," present tense, right now. You are already immortal. Jesus promised that "everyone who lives and believes in me shall never die" (John 11:26). We simply step from time into eternity, from this life to the next.

Nowhere does the Bible say how it feels to become the child of God because our feelings can depend on the pizza we had for supper or the weather outside the window. No circumstances or events can guarantee our salvation. It takes as much faith to believe we are Christians today as it did to become believers. We still have not seen God or proven our salvation in a test tube. If we had, we could question the reality or veracity of what we saw or thought. Either the Bible is true, or it is false. Either God keeps his word, or he does not. He promises that if you "believe in the name of the Son of God," you "have eternal life" this moment. You cannot lose your salvation, for you are already the immortal child of God. This is the fact of God's word.

What about "falling from grace"?

Those who believe that it is possible to trust in Christ and then lose our salvation are quick to quote Hebrews 6:4–6. These interpreters assume that the text speaks of people who have experienced a genuine conversion then "fall away" (v. 6). They typically believe that such a person needs another salvation experience.

But others disagree. Some believe that the writer is stating a hypothetical case: If genuine Christians "have fallen away," then "it is impossible" for them to be brought back to repentance (vv. 4, 6). Not that they can actually fall from salvation, but, if they could, they could not be saved again. Note that if the text deals with a Christian who actually falls from faith, it teaches that the person has no chance to be saved again.

Others believe that the writer is speaking not of a Christian but of someone who considers the faith, perhaps even joins a church, but then rejects Christ. If such a person persists in unbelief, he cannot then be saved. If a person claims that he once trusted Christ but does so no more, we would believe that he was never a genuine Christian.

The Bible seems clearly to teach that a Christian is forever the child of God:

- "For God so loved the world, that he gave his only Son, that whoever believes in him should not perish but have eternal life" (John 3:16).

- "If anyone is in Christ, he is a new creation: The old has passed away; behold, the new has come" (2 Corinthians 5:17).

- "My sheep hear my voice, and I know them, and they follow me. I give them eternal life, and they will never perish, and no one will snatch them out of my hand. My Father, who has given them to me, is greater than all, and no one can snatch them out of my Father's hand" (John 10:27–29).

- "Everyone who lives and believes in me shall never die" (John 11:26).

What about the "unpardonable sin"?

Jesus has just healed a demon-possessed man. The crowds think he might be the Messiah, but the Pharisees say that he drives out demons by the devil himself. So, Jesus responds, "Blasphemy against the Spirit will not be forgiven" (Matthew 12:31). He repeats his warning: "Whoever speaks a word against the Son of Man will be forgiven, but whoever speaks against the Holy Spirit will not be forgiven, either in this age or in the age to come" (v. 32).

Peter could deny Jesus, Thomas could doubt him, and Paul

could persecute his followers, yet they could be forgiven. But "blasphemy against the Spirit" cannot be forgiven, now or at any point in the future. This is the "unpardonable sin." So, what is this sin? Let's set out what we know.

We know that Christians cannot commit this sin. The Bible is clear in 1 John 1:9: "If we confess our sins, he is faithful and just to forgive us our sins and to cleanse us from all unrighteousness." "All" means all. No sin is unpardonable for a Christian.

We know that this sin relates to the work of the Holy Spirit in regard to unbelievers. Jesus is warning the Pharisees, those who rejected him, that they are in danger of this sin. So, what does the Spirit do with non-Christians?

- He convicts them of their sin and need for salvation: "When [the Spirit] comes, he will convict the world concerning sin and righteousness and judgment" (John 16:8).

- He tells them about Christ their Savior: "When the Helper comes, whom I will send to you from the Father, the Spirit of truth, who proceeds from the Father, he will bear witness about me" (John 15:26).

- He explains salvation: "The natural person does not accept the things of the Spirit of God, for they are folly to him, and he is not able to understand them because they are spiritually discerned" (1 Corinthians 2:14).

- When they confess their sins and turn to Christ, the Spirit makes them God's children: "Anyone who does not have the Spirit of Christ does not belong to him. . . . If the Spirit of him who raised Jesus from the dead dwells in you, he who raised Christ Jesus from the dead will also give life to your mortal bodies through his Spirit who lives in you" (Romans 8:9, 11).

In short, the Holy Spirit leads lost people to salvation.

So, we know that it is the "unpardonable sin" to refuse the Spirit's work in leading you to salvation. To be convicted of your sin and need for a savior but refuse to admit it. To be presented the gospel but reject it. Why is this sin unpardonable? Because accepting salvation through Christ is the only means by which our sins can be pardoned.

It is "unpardonable" to reject the only surgery that can save your life or the only chemotherapy that can cure your cancer. Not because the doctor doesn't want to heal you, but because he cannot. You won't let him. You have rejected the only means of health and salvation. The unpardonable sin is rejecting the Holy Spirit's offer of salvation and dying in such a state of rejection. Then you have refused the only pardon God is able to give you. Don't do that. Be sure you have made Christ your Lord, today.

To conclude this part of our conversation: no verse of Scripture connects suicide with our eternal destiny. If this act could cause us to lose our salvation, we believe the Bible would make that fact clear. On the contrary, we can neither earn nor lose our salvation by human actions: "For by grace you have been saved through faith. And this is not your own doing; it is the gift of God, not a result of works, so that no one may boast" (Ephesians 2:8–9).

Suicide is a tragedy for all involved, including our Father in heaven. But the Bible nowhere teaches that it costs Christians their salvation.

SUICIDE AND PHYSICIAN-ASSISTED DEATH

Physician-assisted death (PAD), or euthanasia, is legal in nine US states and the District of Columbia. Said differently, PAD is available to one in five Americans today. We can expect the push for PAD to increase in the future. A 2018 Gallup poll found that nearly seven in ten Americans (72 percent) said "doctors should be allowed by law to end the patient's life by some painless means if the patient and his or her family request it."

Euthanasia terms and concepts

"Euthanasia" is derived from the Greek words *eu* (well) and *thanatos* (death). The term usually means "a good death" or "mercy killing" and is understood to be the provision of an easy, painless death to one who suffers from an incurable or extremely painful affliction.

Types of euthanasia

A distinction is usually made between "active" and "passive" euthanasia:

- Active euthanasia occurs when someone acts to produce death. This is often called "assisted suicide," as in the actions of doctors who provide medical intervention leading directly to death (such as the use of fatal injections).

- "Passive" euthanasia occurs when the patient is treated (or not treated) in a way that is intended to lead to death, but actions are not taken to cause death directly (withholding sustenance, for example).

A third category has become common in recent years. "Letting die" refers to medical actions taken to enhance the patient's well-being during the dying process. Unlike passive euthanasia, the doctor does not intend the patient to die as a result of this decision. Rather, the doctor withholds medical treatments that intensify suffering or merely postpone the moment of death for a short time. For instance, it is not considered passive euthanasia to discontinue chemotherapy in cases of advanced cancer, especially if the drugs increase the suffering of the patient. Nor is it active or passive euthanasia to elevate levels of morphine or similar medications to alleviate suffering, even if the patient may die more quickly as a result. In such cases, the physician does not intend this decision to cause death, even though death may result from his or her action.

Relevant terms

The decision to enact euthanasia is termed "non-voluntary" when patients cannot express their wishes. It would be considered "involuntary" by any who believe that it goes against the patient's wishes as he or she would have expressed them. A patient's euthanized death would be "voluntary" if he or she gave "informed consent" while motivated by his or her best interests (unlike a person suffering from mental or emotional illness who wishes to die).

A patient who executes a "durable power of attorney" assigns responsibility for medical decisions to another person, usually the spouse. In the absence of such an action, the court often assigns responsibility to the spouse, a decision known as "substituted judgment."

Using life support and/or similar technology to maintain a patient's life is termed "heroic" or "extraordinary measures." Some patients wish only "ordinary means" that offer a reasonable hope of benefit and are not excessively burdensome. A third means of support could be called "basic," providing only nutrition and water.

Doctors are required to help their patients ("beneficence") and to refrain from harming them ("non-maleficence"). They can ethically provide medical assistance to alleviate any suffering, even if such help shortens their patients' lives. This "double effect principle" assures that doctors do not act immorally if they intend only the good effect, do not use bad as a means to good, and create good at least equal to the bad. For example, as stated earlier, doctors can prescribe morphine to alleviate the suffering of a terminally ill patient, even if a side effect of morphine in that patient will shorten the person's life—unless they intend the drug to shorten or end that life.

Definitions of "death"

Doctors usually consider "death" to occur when circulation or respiration ceases irreversibly, or when the whole brain does the same. "Brain death" is a special category. The "upper brain" supports consciousness, while the brain stem controls body functions such as breathing and heart rate. If the upper brain has died, the patient is considered to be in a "persistent vegetative state" (PVS). There are estimated to be 10,000 to 25,000 PVS patients in the United States. If the brain stem has also died, the patient is considered to have suffered "brain death." Because nerve cells do not regenerate, both upper-brain and total brain death are completely irreversible.

Biblical options

At the outset, let's make it clear that active euthanasia or "assisted suicide" is unbiblical. This practice is the overt, intentional taking of life and is prohibited by the Sixth Commandment. For the remainder of this section, we will consider euthanasia only as the subject relates to passive or "letting die" options.

Defining the alternatives

Many ethicists believe that in cases of total brain death or upper-brain death, "heroic" measures are unnecessary. Many believe that ordinary treatment is not obligatory and "letting die" is moral. Some, however, believe that it is wrong to withdraw food and hydration, allowing the body to starve. This approach views the life as "holistic," meaning that a functioning body is still united to the "soul," the "image of God." Such a person is still a member of the human race and deserves at least basic care (food and water), if not ordinary care (routine medical support).

Other Christians believe that brain-dead or PVS patients are simply bodies, that their souls or spiritual selves have gone on to eternity. Withdrawing food and water from such patients is then considered to be morally acceptable. In this view, without a functioning brain, the body no longer sustains a soul or retains the image of God. Medical personnel should always care for those who possess the potential for conscious life. But when a PVS exists, there is no possibility of brain regeneration and the "soul" has left the body.

Still others support "vitalism," the belief that physical function by itself is sacred. In this view, even if the "soul" has departed a body that is brain-dead or in a PVS, the body deserves medical treatment to the very end of physical life. Some "vitalists" support ordinary care or basic care for such a body, while others argue for heroic means to preserve physical function as long as possible.

Which view is the most biblical?

Created in the image of God

One way to answer our question involves the scriptural description of humanity as created "in God's image."

Genesis says that "God created man in his own image, in the image of God he created him; male and female he created them" (Genesis 1:27). What does it mean to be made in God's "image"?

Most theologians focus on humanity's uniqueness. What is it that separates us from other forms of life? Such characteristics make us uniquely "the image of God." Four biblical statements address the question:

- We are created in God's image to "have dominion over" his creation (Genesis 1:28).

- The Lord warns us, "Whoever sheds the blood of man, by man shall his blood be shed, for God made man in his own image" (Genesis 9:6).

- Paul states that a man is "the image and glory of God" (1 Corinthians 11:7).

- James states that people are "made in the likeness of God" (James 3:9).

From these specific biblical references to the "image" or "likeness" of God, we can suggest that a person retains this "image" when he or she is able to relate to the rest of God's creation as his representative on earth. We are to "rule" or govern creation, represent God to others, and value each other. In this sense, we are "in" his image so long as we manifest his image on earth. By this reasoning, we lose the "image of God," that which makes us uniquely human and valuable, when we lose the ability or potential to relate to ourselves, our environment, other humans, and God. A baby in the womb and a comatose patient are each a person in that they retain the potential for such interaction. But a PVS individual is not.

Dualistic and holistic views

How does this distinction relate to the body?

Some believe that the "soul" can depart the body before its physical death. This is typically considered the "dualistic" view, separating the physical and the spiritual. Jesus cried from the cross, "Father, into your hands I commit my spirit!" (Luke 23:46). Stephen prayed before his physical death, "Lord Jesus, receive my spirit" (Acts 7:59). Some interpreters use these statements to separate the soul or "image of God" from the body. In the belief that a PVS patient does not and cannot exhibit the image of God, it is then concluded that the person's "soul" has left the body. Any physical support for the body, even food and water, is thus unnecessary.

Others adopt a holistic understanding of the biblical view of humans. While Greek philosophy separated body, soul, and spirit, Hebrew theology did not. It is not that we *have* a body, soul, and spirit that can be identified as separate entities. Rather, we *are* body, soul, and spirit. These words are different dimensions of the one person (cf. 1 Thessalonians 5:23). In the holistic view, we retain the "image of God" so long as our bodies retain some dimension of physical life. In this approach, so long as a person is alive physically, that person is the "image of God." Food and water would be essential, appropriate provision for any person. And so, the decision to withdraw food and water would be wrong.

Permission to die?

What if a patient previously directed that such withdrawal occur? Then the law would require that his or her wishes be honored. But should it? Should we be permitted to mandate that heroic or even ordinary measures *not* be taken to maintain our lives?

The dualistic view believes that a patient loses the "image of God" in certain medical conditions and would support that person's previously stated right to refuse medical life support. The holistic view, taken to its logical conclusion, would seem to require at least food and water to be provided in the desire to preserve and honor the "image of God." It could be argued that even heroic measures are required and that a person should not be allowed to refuse them. Just as we require passengers in cars and airplanes to wear seat belts, so we should require patients to receive all medical support for as long as their bodies survive.

My position

I believe that the holistic view reflects God's understanding of humanity. But I also believe a distinction between heroic, ordinary, and basic life support is warranted. In my view, it is permissible to cease heroic or even ordinary life support for a person who possesses no actual or potential capacity for relational life on any level, as that person cannot demonstrate the "image of God." But I also believe that, so long as the body is alive, the "person" is alive. And persons deserve at least basic support (food and water) for as long as they live.

However, we and/or our doctors can choose to "let die," to take medical steps that do not prolong our lives. When these medical actions enhance the present quality of life, even if they shorten the life span of terminally ill patients, they are especially warranted.

Medical care and the power of God

In dealing with family members facing end-of-life decisions, here are the questions I think we should ask:

- Do they intend to hasten or even cause death? I do not believe such a decision is defensible.

- On the other hand, do they wish simply to allow nature to take over, "letting die" if this is the natural result of the patient's condition? In this situation, medical support is not prolonging life—it is prolonging death.

Maintaining or ending medical care does not necessarily affect the intervention of God. The Lord Jesus raised Lazarus from the grave after he had been dead four days (John 11:38–44). God does not require medical life support to heal. And if it is his will that the patient not survive physically, no medical means can defeat his purpose. If all medical options have been exhausted and there is no plausible reason to believe the patient will ever improve, a family who ends heroic or ordinary life support is not removing the possibility of divine intervention. Rather, they are placing their loved one in God's hands, allowing him to heal physically or eternally.

HELP FOR THOSE CONSIDERING SUICIDE

People consider suicide when the pain they feel exceeds their ability to cope with it. They want to end their suffering and think that ending their lives will bring relief. If you or someone you know is having thoughts of suicide, please get help immediately.

Ask your pastor to recommend a Christian counselor in your area. You can call the National Suicide Prevention Lifeline at 1-800-273-8255 (TALK) or go to the National Suicide Prevention Lifeline's website at suicidepreventionlifeline.org. Take every threat of suicide seriously.

In the meanwhile, it is important to know that it is possible to get through this. *Feeling* suicidal does not require that we act on our feeling. The best thing to do immediately is to create some space. If we decide not to act on our feelings for even a few minutes or a day, we can find the strength to seek help. By seeking help, we can deal with the pain and find the hope we need.

Warning signs

The Centers for Disease Control lists these twelve "suicide warning signs":

- Feeling like a burden

- Being isolated

- Increased anxiety

- Feeling trapped or in unbearable pain

- Increased substance use

- Looking for a way to access lethal means

- Increased anger or rage

- Extreme mood swings

- Expressing hopelessness

- Sleeping too little or too much

- Talking or posting about wanting to die

- Making plans for suicide

This is an issue parents need to discuss with their children too. In Janet Denison's article on JanetDenison.org, "The Kate Spade Conversation," she discusses the major rise in depression among teenagers and links to an important article by the Society to Prevent Teenage Suicide. And she notes that "too often, Christians feel that depression should simply be handled 'spiritually' instead of 'medically.' Depression is an illness, and an illness needs both types of help. If you have reason to believe your child is clinically depressed, you and your child need the help of a physician, as well as the Great Physician."

Protective factors

The following indicators help buffer people from the risks associated with suicide:

- Effective clinical care for mental, physical, and substance abuse disorders

- Easy access to clinical interventions and support for those seeking help

- Family and community support

- Support from ongoing medical and mental health care relationships

- Skills in problem-solving, conflict resolution, and nonviolent ways of handling disputes

- Cultural and religious beliefs that discourage suicide and encourage self-preservation instincts

Help those you care about to experience these positive influences and you'll do much to prevent the tragedy of suicide.

THREE BIBLICAL PROMISES

In the appendix of his classic book, *The Problem of Pain*, C. S. Lewis includes this note from physician R. Havard: "Mental pain is less dramatic than physical pain, but it is more common and also more hard to bear. The frequent attempt to conceal mental pain increases the burden: it is easier to say 'My tooth is aching' than to say 'My heart is broken.'"

Let's close by claiming three promises God makes to every suffering person today.

One: You and every person you know is someone of inestimable worth.

Depression and life crises can cause us to feel that our lives are not worth living. The opposite is true. Every person on earth is someone for whom Jesus died (Romans 5:8). In 1941, C. S. Lewis preached his famous "Weight of Glory" sermon in St. Mary's Chapel at Oxford University. In it, he stated, "There are no *ordinary* people. You have never talked to a mere mortal. Nations, cultures, arts, civilizations—these are mortal, and their life is to ours as the life of a gnat" (his emphasis). Lewis adds: "Next to the Blessed Sacrament itself, your neighbor is the holiest object presented to your senses." So are you.

Two: God loves you and wants to help.

When Elijah despaired of his life and prayed, "It is enough; now, O Lord, take away my life" (1 Kings 19:4), God provided the physical, spiritual, and emotional sustenance he needed to go on. When Jeremiah said, "Cursed be the day on I was born!" (Jeremiah 20:14), God sustained his prophet. Scripture promises: "The Lord is near to the brokenhearted and saves the crushed in spirit" (Psalm 34:18). Paul, who faced almost indescribable challenges (2 Corinthians 11:23–28), could proclaim, "I consider the sufferings of this present time are not worth comparing with the glory that is to be revealed to us" (Romans 8:18).

Jesus knows your pain. He has faced everything we face (Hebrews 4:15). He cried from the cross, "My God, my God, why have you forsaken me?" (Matthew 27:46). Now he is ready to help you. However, let me repeat that one of the most important ways the Great Physician heals is through human physicians. That's why you need to reach out to professional counselors as soon as possible. God will use them as he ministers his grace to you.

Three: You can "dwell on the heights" with God.

Paul testified that he could "take every thought captive to obey Christ" (2 Corinthians 10:5). He could do this because he lived in the power of the Holy Spirit (Ephesians 5:18). God wants to be "the stability of your times, abundance of salvation, wisdom and knowledge" (Isaiah 33:6). The person who walks with him "will dwell on the heights" (v. 16). You can "dwell on the heights" with your Father. This is the promise, and the invitation, of God.

Will you accept it today?

A DISCUSSION GUIDE ON SUICIDE

The following discussion guide may be used in a small group setting or for your personal time of devotion. We hope it helps you both better understand the topic and how God might want to use you, in your specific context, to be "salt and light" on this issue. A PDF download is available at denisonforum.org/courage-questions.

NOTE: If you or someone you know is having thoughts of suicide, please get help immediately. Ask your pastor to recommend a Christian counselor in your area. You can call the National Suicide Prevention Lifeline at 1-800-273-8255 (TALK) or go to the National Suicide Prevention Lifeline's website at suicidepreventionlifeline.org. Take every threat of suicide seriously.

1. When a famous person dies by suicide, how does it make you feel?

2. Have you ever experienced someone close to you dying by suicide? How did you react? What do you wish you would have known or done before their decision?

3. Does our culture accept suicide? What evidence proves your stance?

4. What have you learned in church about suicide?

5. Do you believe that a Christian who commits suicide will enter heaven? What biblical proof can you cite?

6. How does the question of "the unpardonable sin" relate to whether a Christian can lose his or her salvation? Put another way, can a Christian "fall from grace"?

7. Does our culture accept physician-assisted suicide? What evidence proves your stance?

8. Have you ever given thought to what "extreme measures" you would allow to yourself if placed in a medically precarious position? Or have you had a personal experience with family or friends facing such decisions? How did they decide their chosen path?

9. If you had an aggressive disease and had been given only months to live, would you seek quantity of life or quality of life? Why?

10. What does it mean to be created in God's image? How does this fact relate to physician-assisted suicide?

11. How do the dualistic and holistic views of the body differ?

12. How can you help others dealing with anxiety, depression, and/or thoughts of suicide?

13. What are three promises of God every Christian can claim when it comes to the problem of suicide?

ABOUT THE AUTHOR

DR. JIM DENISON is the Chief Vision Officer and founder of the Denison Forum. Through The Daily Article, his email newsletter and podcast that reaches a global audience, Dr. Denison guides readers to discern today's news—biblically.

He is the author of multiple books and has taught philosophy of religion and apologetics at several seminaries. He is the Resident Scholar for Ethics with Baylor Scott & White Health, a Senior Fellow with the 21st Century Wilberforce Initiative, and a Senior Fellow for Global Studies at Dallas Baptist University's Institute for Global Engagement.

Dr. Denison holds a Ph.D. and M.Div. from Southwestern Baptist Theological Seminary, as well as a Doctor of Divinity from Dallas Baptist University. Prior to launching Denison Ministries, he pastored churches in Texas and Georgia. Jim and his wife, Janet, live in Dallas, Texas. They have two sons and four grandchildren.

ABOUT DENISON MINISTRIES

DENISON MINISTRIES exists to create culture-changing Christians who are committed to advancing the kingdom through that sphere of influence.

We aspire to influence 3 million Christians every day to experience God through a daily devotional resource (First15.org), to speak into real life through daily cultural commentary (DenisonForum.org), and to bring Jesus into parenting moments (ChristianParenting.org).

Learn more at DenisonMinistries.org.

NOTES

FOREWORD

01   **"Jesus Christ . . . was not perfect":** Julio Rosas, "Don Lemon Asserts Jesus Christ 'Was Not Perfect' While He Was on Earth," Video, 2:45, https://www.youtube.com/watch?v=21Sbaiu89S0.

01   **"reexamine themselves and their teachings":** Hank Berrien, "'Reexamine Themselves And Their Teachings': Don Lemon Attacks Vatican For Refusing To Bless Same-Sex Unions," The Daily Wire, last modified March 15, 2021, https://www.dailywire.com/news/reexamine-themselves-and-their-teachings-don-lemon-attacks-vatican-for-refusing-to-bless-same-sex-unions.

02   **"I respect people's right to believe":** Berrien.

1. THE GREATEST SIN IN AMERICA: WHAT DOES THE BIBLE SAY ABOUT RACISM?

06   **"a unique anxiety":** Matthew Futterman and Talya Minsberg, "After a Killing, 'Running While Black' Stirs Even More Anxiety," *New York Times*, last modified May 26, 2020, https://www.nytimes.com/2020/05/08/sports/Ahmaud-Arbery-running.html.

06   **"a majority of Americans":** Juliana Menasce Horowitz, Anna Brown, and Kiana Cox, "How Americans see the state of race relations,"

Pew Research Center, last modified April 9,
2019, https://www.pewresearch.org/social-
trends/2019/04/09/how-americans-see-the-state-
of-race-relations/

06   **60 percent of hate crimes:** "2016 Hate Crime
Statistics Released," FBI, last modified November
13, 2017, https://www.fbi.gov/news/stories/2016-
hate-crime-statistics.

07   **"prejudice, discrimination, or antagonism":**
"racism," Lexico, https://www.lexico.com/
definition/racism.

07   **"having little of Humanitie":** Sean P.
Harvey, "Ideas of Race in Early America,"
Oxford Research Encyclopedias: American
History, last modified April 5, 2016, https://
oxfordre.com/americanhistory/view/10.1093/
acrefore/9780199329175.001.0001/acrefore-
9780199329175-e-262.

07   **"Negro's were Beasts":** Harvey.

08   **"There were four million slaves":** Aaron
O'Neill, "Black and slave population of the United
States from 1790 to 1880," statista, last modified
March 19, 2021, https://www.statista.com/
statistics/1010169/black-and-slave-population-
us-1790-1880/.

09   **"a 50-percent rise in coverage of anti-Asian
racism":** Kate Shellnut, "Asian Americans Call
on the Church to Preach Against Coronavirus
Racism," *Christianity Today*, last modified March
31, 2020, https://www.christianitytoday.com/
news/2020/march/asian-american-christian-

statement-coronavirus-racism.html.

10   **Studies show that racism persists in America:** Jeff Nesbit, "Institutional Racism Is Our Way of Life," *U.S. News & World Report*, last modified May 6, 2015, https://www.usnews.com/news/blogs/at-the-edge/2015/05/06/institutional-racism-is-our-way-of-life.

10   **"my church is involved with racial reconciliation":** Ruth Moon, "Does the Gospel Mandate Racial Reconciliation? White Pastors Agree More Than Black Pastors," *Christianity Today*, last modified December 16, 2014, https://www.christianitytoday.com/news/2014/december/does-gospel-mandate-racial-reconciliation-lifeway-kainos.html.

10   **"people of color are often put at a social disadvantage":** "people of color are often put at a social disadvantage," Barna, last modified May 5, 2016, https://www.barna.com/research/black-lives-matter-and-racial-tension-in-america/#.V45Hf5MrKb8.

11   **81 percent of America's Protestant churches:** Bob Smietana, "Sunday Morning Segregation: Most Worshipers Feel Their Church Has Enough Diversity," *Christianity Today*, last modified January 15, 2015, https://www.christianitytoday.com/news/2015/january/sunday-morning-segregation-most-worshipers-church-diversity.html.

11   **90 percent of Protestant pastors:** Smietana.

15   **"We know many among ourselves":** Pope
      Saint Clement I, trans. by Alexander Roberts and
      James Donaldson, "First Epistle to the Corinthians,"
      Ch. 55, Logos Library, http://www.logoslibrary.
      org/clement1/corinthians/55.html.

15   **"Do not despise either male or female
      slaves":** "St. Ignatius of Antiocha To Polycarp,
      Chapter IV-Exhortations," The epistle to Polycarp,
      IntraText, http://www.intratext.com/IXT/
      ENG0861/_P5.HTM.

21   **As Dr. Evans shows:** Tony Evans, "Are Black
      People Cursed? The Curse of Ham," eternal
      perspective ministries, last modified January 18,
      2010, https://www.epm.org/resources/2010/
      Jan/18/are-black-people-cursed-curse-ham/.

23   **64 percent of Americans:** Andrew Arenge,
      Stephanie Perry and Dartunorro Clark, "Poll: 64
      percent of Americans say racism remains a major
      problem," NBC News, last modified May 29, 2018,
      https://www.nbcnews.com/politics/politics-news/
      poll-64-percent-americans-say-racism-remains-
      major-problem-n877536.

24   **"In some ways, it's super simple":** William
      Wan and Sarah Kaplan, "Why are people still
      racist? What science says about America's race
      problem.," *Washington Post*, last modified August 14,
      2017, https://www.washingtonpost.com/news/
      speaking-of-science/wp/2017/08/14/why-are-
      people-still-racist-what-science-says-about-americas-
      race-problem/.

25   **"Americans, I think, have a great
      advantage":** Julissa Higgins, "Read George W.

Bush's Speech at the Dallas Shooting Memorial Service," *Time*, last modified July 12, 2016, https://time.com/4403510/george-w-bush-speech-dallas-shooting-memorial-service/.

26 **"One of the real tragedies today":** Tony Evans, "Opinion: America's current violence can be traced to Christians' failures," *Washington Post*, last modified July 9, 2016, https://www.washingtonpost.com/news/acts-of-faith/wp/2016/07/09/americas-current-violence-can-be-traced-to-christians-failures/.

26 **"We who hated and destroyed":** Justin Martyr, "The First Apology," New Advent, https://www.newadvent.org/fathers/0126.htm.

27 **"Through the perfection of his love":** Mayor, Joseph Bickersteth., Hort, Fenton John Anthony. Clement of Alexandria, *Miscellanies Book VII: The Greek Text with Introduction, Translation, Notes, Dissertations and Indices* (United Kingdom: Macmillan, 1902), 135.

27 **"We love one another":** Minucius Felix, "Ante-Nicene Fathers, Vol IV: The Octavius of Minucius Felix.," St-Takla.org: Coptic Orthodox Church Heritage, https://st-takla.org/books/en/ecf/004/0040034.html.

27 **"See how they love one another":** Christianity.com Editorial Staff, "What Were Early Christians Like?," Christianity.com, last modified May 3, 2010, https://www.christianity.com/church/church-history/timeline/1-300/what-were-early-christians-like-11629560.html.

2. THE MORAL ISSUE OF OUR TIME: WHAT DOES THE BIBLE SAY ABOUT ABORTION?

31   **more than thirty-six thousand people die on US highways:** "Traffic Deaths Decreased in 2018, but Still 36,560 People Died," United States Department of Transportation: NHTSA, https://www.nhtsa.gov/traffic-deaths-2018.

31   **more than sixty-one million abortions:** "Abortion statistics: United States Data and Trends," National Right to Life, https://nrlc.org/uploads/factsheets/FS01AbortionintheUS.pdf.

32   **almost 620,000 abortions**: "CDCs Abortion Surveillance System FAQs," Centers for Disease Control and Prevention, last modified November 25, 2020, https://www.cdc.gov/reproductivehealth/data_stats/abortion.htm.

34   **several specific reasons why she might choose abortion:** "Roe v. Wade / Excerpts from Majority Opinion," Landmark Cases, last modified August 20, 2020, https://www.landmarkcases.org/assets/site_18/files/roe_v_wade/teacher/pdf/decision_majority_excerpts_roe_teacher.pdf.

42   **"The embryo has its own autonomy":** Karl Barth, *Church Dogmatics* (Edinburgh: T & T Clark, 1985 [1961]) 3.4.416.

46   **"The law seems rather to mean":** Flavius Josephus, *The Works of Josephus* (United States: Lindsay & Blakiston, 1859), 314.

54   **abortion must be legal as a remedy:** Virginia Ramey Mollenkott, "Reproductive Choice: Basic

to Justice for Women" in *Readings in Christian Ethics: Volume 2: Issues and Applications*, eds. David K. Clark and Robert V. Rakestraw (Baker Academic: 2008).

58   **"Your opinion [in Roe v. Wade] stated":** Mother Teresa in *Speeches that Changed the World* (United States: Westminster John Knox Press, 1999), 431.

58   **"It is a poverty to decide":** "7 of Our Favorite Mother Teresa Quotes," March for Life, last modified August 31, 2017, https://marchforlife. org/mother-teresa-favorite-quotes/.

58   **"the greatest destroyer of peace today":** Mother Teresa of Calcutta, "Whatsoever You Do...": Speech of Mother Teresa of Calcutta to the National Prayer Breakfast, Washington, DC, February 3, 1994, https://www.priestsforlife.org/ library/4386-whatsoever-you-do.

3. THE CALL TO TRANSFORMATIONAL GOOD: WHAT DOES THE BIBLE SAY ABOUT POLITICS?

67   **William Wilberforce experienced a spiritual rebirth:** "William Wilberforce: Antislavery politician," *Christianity Today*, https://www. christianitytoday.com/history/people/activists/ william-wilberforce.html.

68   **"the art or science of government":** "politics," Merriam-Webster, last modified April 7, 2021, https://www.merriam-webster.com/ dictionary/politics.

68   **four kinds of political systems:** "Political

system," Wikipedia, last modified March 31, 2021, https://en.wikipedia.org/wiki/Political_system.

69 **"Politicians are the same all over":**
"Khrushchev Needles Peking," *Chicago Tribune*, August 22, 1963.

71 **nearly all US presidents . . . Christian faith:** Aleksandra Sandstrom, "Biden is only the second Catholic president, but nearly all have been Christians," Pew Research Center, last modified January 20, 2021, https://www.pewresearch.org/fact-tank/2021/01/20/biden-only-second-catholic-president-but-nearly-all-have-been-christians-2/.

73 **China is the world's largest producer of Bibles:** Eleanor Albert, "Christianity in China," Council on Foreign Religions, last modified October 11, 2018, https://www.cfr.org/backgrounder/christianity-china.

73 **more Christians than members of the Communist Party:** Tsukasa Hadano, "China's Christians keep the faith, rattling the country's leaders," Nikkei Asia, last modified September 10, 2019.

73 **"more Protestants in church in China than in all of Europe":** Serene Fang, "A Brief History of the Christianity in China," Frontline/World, https://www.pbs.org/frontlineworld/stories/china_705/history/china.html.

78 **"The propitious smiles of heaven":** George Washington, "Washington's Inaugural Address of 1789," National Archives and Records Administration, https://www.archives.gov/exhibits/american_originals/inaugtxt.html.

4. THE OPPORTUNITY TO ENGAGE CULTURE: WHAT DOES THE BIBLE SAY ABOUT RELIGIOUS LIBERTY?

81   **"Fighting to take the position":** "The hill you want to die on," Grammarist, https://grammarist.com/idiom/the-hill-you-want-to-die-on/.

82   **"Singing in church is a biblical mandate":** Chace Beech, "Three California churches sue Newsom over singing ban," *Los Angeles Times*, last modified July 16, 2020, https://www.latimes.com/california/story/2020-07-16/california-churches-sue-newsom-singing-ban.

82   **a video of his sermon**: Grace to You, "We Must Obey God Rather Than Men," YouTube, last modified July 28, 2020, https://www.youtube.com/watch?v=t2ixUp5KKn8.

82   **"the biblical mandate to gather for corporate worship":** "Christ, not Caesar, Is Head of the Church," Grace Community Church, last modified December 11, 2020, https://www.gracechurch.org/news/posts/1988.

82   ***South Bay United Pentecostal Church v. Newsom***: Supreme Court of the United States, "SOUTH BAY UNITED PENTECOSTAL CHURCH, ET AL. v. GAVIN NEWSOM, GOVERNOR OF CALIFORNIA, ET AL," last modified May 29, 2020, https://www.supremecourt.gov/opinions/19pdf/19a1044_pok0.pdf.

83   ***Calvary Chapel Dayton Valley v. Sisolak***: Supreme Court of the United States, CALVARY

CHAPEL DAYTON VALLEY v. STEVE SISOLAK, GOVERNOR OF NEVADA, ET AL., last modified July 24, 2020, https://www.supremecourt.gov/opinions/19pdf/19a1070_0811.pdf.

84   **"It's an ideal setting for transmission":** Kate Conger, Jack Healy and Lucy Tompkins, "Churches Were Eager to Reopen. Now They Are Confronting Coronavirus Cases.," *New York Times*, last modified July 10, 2020, https://www.nytimes.com/2020/07/08/us/coronavirus-churches-outbreaks.html?searchResultPosition=3.

84   **singing in public was especially dangerous:** Kate Hannigan, "Is Singing in a Choir Safe During COVID-19? A Voice Expert Explains the Risk," Mass General Brigham: Mass Eye and Ear: focus, last modified May 21, 2020, https://focus.masseyeandear.org/is-singing-in-a-choir-safe-during-covid-19-a-voice-expert-explains-the-risk/.

84   **One choir in Washington:** Laura Geggel, "How a superspreader at choir practice sickened 52 people with COVID-19," Live Science, last modified May 14, 2020, https://www.livescience.com/covid-19-superspreader-singing.html.

85   **Nevada wants to "jump-start business activity":** Supreme Court of the United States, CALVARY CHAPEL DAYTON VALLEY v. STEVE SISOLAK, GOVERNOR OF NEVADA, ET AL., last modified July 24, 2020, https://www.supremecourt.gov/opinions/19pdf/19a1070_0811.pdf.

85   **enormous economic benefits:** Kelsey Dallas, "Economic impact of religion: New report

says it's worth more than Google, Apple and Amazon combined," *Desert News*, last modified September 14, 2016, https://www.deseret.com/2016/9/14/20596145/economic-impact-of-religion-new-report-says-it-s-worth-more-than-google-apple-and-amazon-combined#a-first-of-its-kind-analysis-of-religions-socio-economic-value-shows-that-faith-related-businesses-and-institutions-add-more-than-1-trillion-to-the-u-s-economy.

85   **"The Bill of Rights exists to protect minorities":** Henry Olsen, "Opinion: John Roberts strikes again. Conservatives should be furious.," *Washington Post*, last modified July 27, 2020, https://www.washingtonpost.com/opinions/2020/07/27/john-roberts-strikes-again-conservatives-should-be-furious/.

85   **"For those churches that gather Sunday":** Ed Stetzer, "We Can't Roll the Dice on Religious Liberty: Nevada, the Supreme Court, and Churches," *Christianity Today*, last modified July 25, 2020, https://www.christianitytoday.com/edstetzer/2020/july/nevada-supreme-court-churches-casinos.html.

87   **Lily Damtew decided to close her coffee shop:** Emily Davies, "Two D.C.-area restaurant employees were assaulted after enforcing mask rules. Others worry they will be next.," *Washington Post*, last modified July 13, 2020, https://www.washingtonpost.com/local/two-dc-area-restaurant-employees-were-assaulted-for-enforcing-mask-rules-others-worry-they-will-be-next/2020/07/13/3efcf466-c2c9-11ea-9fdd-b7ac6b051dc8_story.html.

87 **A Family Dollar security guard in Flint, Michigan:** Meryl Kornfield, "Three people charged in killing of Family Dollar security guard over mask policy," *Washington Post*, last modified May 5, 2020, https://www.washingtonpost.com/nation/2020/05/04/security-guards-death-might-have-been-because-he-wouldnt-let-woman-store-without-mask/.

87 **A Starbucks worker was denounced on social media:** Sydney Page, "On Facebook, she denounced a Starbucks worker who asked her to wear a mask. It backfired: He received over $32,000 in tips.," *Washington Post*, last modified June 26, 2020, https://www.washingtonpost.com/lifestyle/2020/06/26/facebook-she-denounced-starbucks-worker-who-asked-her-wear-mask-it-backfired-he-got-26000-tips/.

87 **"the new American pastime":** Jonah E. Bromwich, "Fighting Over Masks in Public Is the New American Pastime," *New York Times*, last modified July 21, 2020, https://www.nytimes.com/2020/06/30/style/mask-america-freedom-coronavirus.html.

87 **why wearing masks is so important during the pandemic:** Dr. Jim Denison, "President Trump says, 'I'm all for masks': Why wearing masks is a vital way to love our neighbor," Denison Forum, last modified July 3, 2020, https://www.denisonforum.org/columns/daily-article/president-trump-says-im-all-for-masks-why-wearing-masks-is-a-vital-way-to-love-our-neighbor/.

87 **"There's really nothing you can do to hide from the virus":** Tara McKelvey, "Coronavirus: Why are Americans so angry about masks?," BBC News, last modified July 20, 2020, https://www.bbc.com/news/world-us-canada-53477121.

88 **exempted religious officiants and worship participants from mask-wearing mandates:** Kelsey Dallas, "Should churches be excluded from mask mandates?," *Desert News*, last modified July 16, 2020, https://www.deseret.com/indepth/2020/7/16/21316033/coronavirus-texas-mask-mandates-religious-exemptions-church-outbreaks-religious-freedom.

88 **"I think people would be really discouraged":** Carla Hinton, "Religious leaders weigh in on mask mandate's exemption for religious gatherings," *The Oklahoman*, last modified July 19, 2020, https://www.oklahoman.com/article/5667070/religious-leaders-weigh-in-on-mask-mandates-exemption-for-religious-gatherings.

88 **Christians in China say the persecutions . . . are worse:** Gary Lane, "Communists Use COVID as Pretext for Persecution: Xi's China Church Crackdown Worse Than Under Mao," CBN News, last modified July 29, 2020, https://www1.cbn.com/cbnnews/cwn/2020/july/xis-china-church-crackdown-worse-than-under-mao.

88 **"demographic genocide":** The Associated Press, "China cuts Uighur births with IUDs, abortion, sterilization," last modified June 28, 2020, https://apnews.com/article/ap-top-news-international-news-weekend-reads-china-health-269b3de1af34e17c1941a514f78d764c.

88   **Chinese Christians are being pressured to renounce their faith:** Caleb Parke, "Christians see 'alarming' trend worldwide as China builds 'blueprint of persecution'," Fox News, last modified January 15, 2020, https://www.foxnews.com/faith-values/christian-china-persecution-2020-watchlist.

89   **Christians who receive social welfare payments from the Chinese government:** Zhang Feng, "People on Social Welfare Ordered to Worship CCP, Not God," Bitter Winter, last modified July 16, 2020, https://bitterwinter.org/people-on-social-welfare-ordered-to-worship-ccp-not-god/.

89   **"The decentralized, defiant, do-it-your-own-way norms":** Michele Gelfland, "To survive the coronavirus, the United States must tighten up," *Boston Globe*, last modified March 13, 2020, https://www.bostonglobe.com/2020/03/13/opinion/survive-coronavirus-united-states-must-tighten-up/.

90   **"emergency powers are seldom relinquished":** Matthew B. Crawford, "The danger of safteyism," UnHerd, last modified May 15, 2020, https://unherd.com/2020/05/the-hypocrisy-of-safetyism/.

90   **Activists burned a stack of Bibles:** Ian Miles Cheong (@stillgray), "Left-wing activists bring a stack of Bibles to burn in front of the federal courthouse in Portland.," Twitter post, August 1, 2020, https://twitter.com/stillgray/status/1289512762733785088.

90   **A statue of Jesus was beheaded:** Associated Press, "Jesus Statue Beheaded at Catholic Church

in Miami-Dade," NBC Miami, last modified July 17, 2020, https://www.nbcmiami.com/news/local/jesus-statue-beheaded-at-catholic-church-in-miami-dade/2263953/.

90   **faculty survey at Harvard University:** James S. Bikales and Jasper G. Goodman, "Plurality of Surveyed Harvard Faculty Support Warren in Presidential Race," The Harvard Crimson, last modified March 3, 2020, https://www.thecrimson.com/article/2020/3/3/faculty-support-warren-president/.

91   **67 percent of white evangelical Protestants:** "White Evangelicals See Trump as Fighting for Their Beliefs, Though Many Have Mixed Feelings About His Personal Conduct," Pew Research Center, last modified March 12, 2020, https://www.pewforum.org/2020/03/12/white-evangelicals-see-trump-as-fighting-for-their-beliefs-though-many-have-mixed-feelings-about-his-personal-conduct/.

91   **"negative portrayals of Christianity in pop culture":** Mark Silk, "Why white evangelicals are at odds with America," Religion News Service, last modified March 15, 2020, https://religionnews.com/2020/03/15/why-white-evangelicals-are-at-odds-with-america/.

91   **"contains a provision specifically designed to protect the autonomy of religious organizations":** David French, "The True Extent of Religious Liberty in America, Explained," The Dispatch, last modified June 21, 2020, https://frenchpress.thedispatch.com/p/the-true-extent-of-religious-liberty.

98   **ordering Christians to replace images of Jesus:** Kate Shellnutt, "China Tells Christians to Replace Images of Jesus with Communist President," *Christianity Today*, last modified November 17, 2017, https://www.christianitytoday. com/news/2017/november/china-christians-jesus-communist-president-xi-jinping-yugan.html.

5. THE POWER OF HISTORY: WHAT DOES THE BIBLE SAY ABOUT REMOVING STATUES?

103   **"What to the Slave is the Fourth of July?":** Valerie Strauss, "Why this 1852 Frederick Douglass speech — 'What to the Slave Is the Fourth of July?' — should be taught to students today," *New York Times*, last modified July 4, 2020, https://www. washingtonpost.com/education/2020/07/04/why-this-1852-frederick-douglass-speech-what-slave-is-fourth-july-should-be-taught-students-today/.

103   **the statue was torn from its base:** Associated Press, "Frederick Douglass statue vandalized in Rochester park," Yahoo! News, last modified July 5, 2020, https://www.yahoo.com/news/frederick-douglass-statue-vandalized-rochester-001340031. html.

103   **"Statuary Sanctuary City":** Rachel del Guidice, "Ohio Town Announces It's a 'Sanctuary City' for Historical Statues," The Daily Signal, last modified July 6, 2020, https://www.dailysignal. com/2020/07/06/ohio-town-announces-its-a-sanctuary-city-for-historical-statues/.

XX   **154 statues**: Wikipedia, "List of monuments

and memorials removed during the George Floyd protests," https://en.wikipedia.org/wiki/List_of_monuments_and_memorials_removed_during_the_George_Floyd_protests#United_States.

104 **protesters pulled down one such statue:** Associated Press, "Protesters tore down, threw a statue of Christopher Columbus into Baltimore's Inner Harbor," USA Today, last modified July 5, 2020, https://www.usatoday.com/story/news/nation/2020/07/05/christopher-columbus-toppled-thrown-into-baltimores-inner-harbor/5378929002/.

104 **A petition in Cleveland, Ohio:** Audrey Conklin, "Chef Boyardee proposed to replace Christopher Columbus statue," Fox Business, last modified July 3, 2020, https://www.foxbusiness.com/lifestyle/petition-christopher-columbus-chef-boyardee.

104 **Four Confederate statues in Richmond, Virginia**: Ryan W. Miller, "Another Confederate statue in Richmond, Va., comes down along Monument Avenue," Yahoo! News via USA Today, last modified July 7, 2020, https://www.yahoo.com/news/another-confederate-statue-richmond-va-165035795.html.

104 **Columbus, Ohio . . . removed a statue of Columbus:** The Columbus Dispatch, "Christopher Columbus statue removed from Columbus City Hall," USA Today, last modified July 1, 2020, https://www.yahoo.com/news/christopher-columbus-statue-removed-columbus-141811372.html.

105 **"St. Serra made historic sacrifices":** Casey Chalk, "Toppled Statues Of Junipero Serra

Obscure A History Worth Remembering," The Federalist, last modified July 1, 2020, https://thefederalist.com/2020/07/01/toppled-statues-of-junipero-serra-belie-a-history-worth-remembering/.

105 **"Native Americans brought into the mission":** Alejandra Molina, "Who is St. Junipero Serra and why are California protesters toppling his statues?" *America: The Jesuit Review*, last modified June 22, 2020, https://www.americamagazine.org/politics-society/2020/06/22/who-st-junipero-serra-and-why-are-california-protesters-toppling-his.

105 **"I'm a Direct Descendant of Thomas Jefferson.":** Lucian K. Truscott IV, ""I'm a Direct Descendant of Thomas Jefferson. Take Down His Memorial." *New York Times*, last modified July 6, 2020, https://www.nytimes.com/2020/07/06/opinion/thomas-jefferson-memorial-truscott.html.

105 **Stone Mountain . . . has come under special scrutiny:** Jay Busbee, "The story of Stone Mountain, the world's largest Confederate monument," Yahoo! Sports, last modified July 2, 2020, https://sports.yahoo.com/the-story-of-stone-mountain-the-worlds-largest-confederate-monument-160915895.html.

106 **controversy over the Emancipation Memorial at Lincoln Park:** James Hohmann, "The Daily 202: Why a freed slave is kneeling in the Lincoln statue in D.C. that some are trying to remove," *Washington Post*, last modified July 1, 2020, https://www.washingtonpost.com/news/powerpost/paloma/daily-202/2020/07/01/daily-202-why-a-freed-slave-is-kneeling-in-the-lincoln-

statue-in-d-c-that-some-are-trying-to-remove/5efc1
671602ff10807192d1b/.

107   **45 percent of Americans see statues of
      Confederate war heroes:** "The Economist/
      YouGov Poll," YouGov, last modified June 30,
      2020, https://docs.cdn.yougov.com/dhhgae6j8e/
      econToplines.pdf.

107   "**not for what came afterwards**": The
      Dispatch Staff, "The Morning Dispatch: Grappling
      With Our Nation's History," The Dispatch, last
      modified July 6, 2020, https://morning.thedispatch.
      com/p/the-morning-dispatch-grappling-with

107   **"We are watching an organized, coordinated
      campaign":** Tal Axelrod, "South Dakota governor
      criticizes removal of statues as effort to 'discredit'
      nation's principles," The Hill, last modified July
      3, 2020, https://thehill.com/homenews/state-
      watch/505839-south-dakota-governor-criticizes-
      removal-of-statues-as-effort.

107   **threats against the statue of Winston
      Churchill:** Basit Mahmood, "Black Lives
      Matter Protests 'Hijacked by Extremists Intent on
      Violence', Boris Johnson claims," *Newsweek*, last
      modified June 12, 2020, https://www.newsweek.
      com/boris-johnson-black-lives-matter-winston-
      churchill-1510437.

108   **"When you start wiping out your history":**
      Meera Jagannathan, "Condoleezza Rice argues
      tearing down slave owners' statues is 'sanitizing'
      history," *Daily News*, last modified May 8, 2017,
      https://www.nydailynews.com/news/politics/
      condoleezza-rice-argues-removing-slave-owners-
      statues-article-1.3147695.

108 **"It is true that there are monuments":** Tyler Jett, "Without once mentioning the Civil War, Georgia Gov. Brian Kemp signs bill protecting Confederate monuments, other memorials," *Chattanooga Times Free Press*, last modified April 26, 2019, https://www.timesfreepress.com/news/politics/state/story/2019/apr/26/without-mentioning-civil-war-georgia-gov-brian-kemp-signs-bill-protecting-confederate-other-monuments/493534/.

109 **"these statues . . . still retain cultural value":** Catesby Leigh, "Why We Should Keep Confederate Statues Standing," The Federalist, last modified July 1, 2020, https://thefederalist.com/2020/07/01/why-we-should-keep-confederate-statues-standing/.

109 **"As a historian by training":** Timothy Dolan, "Even the Bible Is Full of Flawed Characters," *Wall Street Journal*, last modified June 28, 2020, https://www.wsj.com/articles/even-the-bible-is-full-of-flawed-characters-11593370160.

109 **prosecute individuals who damage statues or monuments:** Andrew Restuccia, "Trump's Executive Order Calls for Limiting Federal Funds to States if They Can't Protect Monuments," *Wall Street Journal*, last modified June 26, 2020, https://www.wsj.com/articles/trump-signs-executive-order-to-increase-penalties-for-damaging-monuments-11593211631.

109 **five different DC laws that are broken:** Cully Stimson, "Criminals Tearing Down DC Statues Should Be Prosecuted. Here Are the Laws They're

Violating.," The Daily Signal, last modified June 24, 2020, https://www.dailysignal.com/2020/06/24/criminals-tearing-down-dc-statues-should-be-prosecuted-here-are-the-laws-theyre-violating/.

110 **"blowing up American culture":** Emily Jashinsky, "Leftists Destroy Abolitionist Statues Because Scorched Cultural Earth Is Their Only Option," The Federalist, last modified July 1, 2020, https://thefederalist.com/2020/07/01/leftists-destroy-abolitionist-statues-because-scorched-cultural-earth-is-their-only-option/.

111 **"Our story is intricately and intimately connected":** Kira Davis, "Do we erase black history when we take down statues?," Spectator, last modified June 26, 2020, https://spectator.us/topic/erase-black-history-take-down-statues/.

111 **"Slave owners should not be honored":** Charles M. Blow, "Yes, Even George Washington," *New York Times*, last modified June 28, 2020, https://www.nytimes.com/2020/06/28/opinion/george-washington-confederate-statues.html.

112 **Joe Biden believes that Confederate monuments belong in museums:** Trevor Hunnicutt, "Biden: Confederate monuments belong in museums, not public squares," Reauters via Yahoo! News, last modified June 30, 2020, https://www.yahoo.com/news/biden-confederate-monuments-belong-museums-190743767.html.

112 **"Erecting statues in honor of white supremacists":** Thomas R. Wells, "The Statues Were Always A Grab For Power," 3 Quarks Daily, last modified June 29, 2020, https://3quarksdaily.

com/3quarksdaily/2020/06/the-statues-were-always-a-grab-for-power.html.

113   **"the great population of statues being destroyed":** James C. McCrery, II, "Confederate Statue-Destroying Mobs Are Doing What Governments Should Have Long Ago," The Federalist, last modified June 29, 2020, https://thefederalist.com/2020/06/29/statue-destroying-mobs-doing-what-governments-should-have-done/.

113   **describes her body as a "Confederate monument":** Caroline Randall Williams, "You Want a Confederate Monument? My Body Is a Confederate Monument," *New York Times*, last modified June 26, 2020, https://www.nytimes.com/2020/06/26/opinion/confederate-monuments-racism.html.

113   **a list of statues they believe should be erected:** Sidney Blumenthal and Sean Wilentz, "Take the statues down. Replace them with any of these people.," *Washington Post*, last modified June 27, 2020, https://www.washingtonpost.com/outlook/2020/06/27/confederate-statues-wpa-reconstruction/.

114   **options to replace Forrest:** Jack Helean, "Dolly Parton statue may replace KKK leader monument at the Tennessee capitol," WCYB, last modified June 14, 2020, https://wcyb.com/news/tennessee-news/dolly-parton-statue-may-replace-kkk-leader-monument-at-the-tennessee-capitol-06-14-2020-111134994.

114   **a threefold approach to the debate over monuments:** Russell Moore, "What's at Stake

with the Confederate Battle Flag," Moore to the Point, https://bit.ly/3fmGN9D

115 **"I have yet to read where anyone suggests":** Randy Baker, "Thomas Jefferson Still Stands — At Least For Now," The Federalist, last modified June 30, 2020, https://thefederalist.com/2020/06/30/thomas-jefferson-still-stands-at-least-for-now/.

115 **calls for removing a statue of St. Louis' namesake:** Associated Press, "Catholic officials defend statue of St. Louis' namesake," AP News, last modified June 28, 2020, https://apnews.com/article/fea7c7a90f4dff6a8e55adb1c68995e4.

116 **"public art had a very clear purpose":** Dr. Anton Howes, "What's the point of statues?," Flink, last modified June 24, 2020, https://fl.ink/explore/whats-the-point-of-statues.

117 **"There can be no doubt that statues of Davis":** Sean Wilentz, "Monuments to a Complicated Past," *Wall Street Journal*, last modified June 25, 2020, https://www.wsj.com/articles/monuments-to-a-complicated-past-11593092992.

117 **"What was the purpose of this monument?":** Jeffrey Collins, "Stop the Vandals, Then Rethink the Monuments," *Wall Street Journal*, last modified June 26, 2020, https://www.wsj.com/articles/stop-the-vandals-then-rethink-the-monuments-11593210991.

121 **"President Franklin Delano Roosevelt worked with segregationists":** Newt Gingrich, "Memory Holes, Mobs, and Speaker Pelosi," Gingrich360, last modified June 19, 2020, https://

www.gingrich360.com/2020/06/19/memory-holes-mobs-and-speaker-pelosi/.

121 **Margaret Sanger . . . "vocal eugenics activist":** Elie Reynolds, "If You Cancel George Washington, You Have To Cancel These 'Progressive Heroes' Too," The Federalist, last modified June 16, 2020, https://thefederalist.com/2020/06/16/if-you-cancel-george-washington-you-have-to-cancel-these-progressive-heroes-too/.

121 **"Even if the ugliest charges against King":** David Greenberg, "How to Make Sense of the Shocking New MLK Documents," Politico, last modified June 4, 2019, https://www.politico.com/magazine/story/2019/06/04/how-to-make-sense-of-the-shocking-new-mlk-documents-227042.

123 **the example of Gen. Robert E. Lee:** Gary W. Gallagher, "Robert E. Lee," Britannica, https://www.britannica.com/biography/Robert-E-Lee.

124 **"not to keep open the sores of war":** Robert E. Lee, Republican Vindicator, September 03, 1869, https://bit.ly/3wCxYhU

125 **Christians took down idolatrous statues across Athens:** Morgan Lee, "Why Christians Have a Reputation for Smashing Statues," *Christianity Today*, last modified July 8, 2020, https://www.christianitytoday.com/ct/podcasts/quick-to-listen/statues-taking-down-christian-history-iconoclasm.html.

126 **"Every man must decide whether":** Martin Luther King Jr., *Strength to Love* Minneapolis: Fortress Press, 2010).

6. THE LATEST EXPRESSION OF THE POSTMODERN CONTRADICTION: WHAT DOES THE BIBLE SAY ABOUT CANCEL CULTURE?

131   **"Introducing women into combat":** Jenny Gross, "Boeing Communications Chief Resigns Over 33-Year-Old Article," *New York Times*, last modified July 8, 2020, https://www.nytimes.com/2020/07/08/business/boeing-resignation-niel-golightly.html.

132   **"Cancel culture":** "What It Means to Get 'Canceled'," Merriam-Webster, last modified January 2021, https://www.merriam-webster.com/words-at-play/cancel-culture-words-were-watching.

132   **editorial page editor:** Brent Lang, "Embattled New York Times Opinion Page Editor James Bennet Resigns," *Variety*, last modified June 7, 2020, https://variety.com/2020/politics/news/new-york-times-james-bennet-tom-cotton-resigns-1234627320/.

132   **professor at UCLA:** Caleb Parke, "White UCLA professor under investigation after reading MLK's 'Letter from Birmingham Jail'," Fox News, last modified June 11, 2020, https://www.foxnews.com/us/ucla-professor-investigation-mlk-n-word.

132   **Jimmy Fallon issued a public apology:** Nadine DeNinno, "Jimmy Fallon apologizes for old blackface skit after viral backlash," *New York Post*, last modified May 26, 2020, https://nypost.com/2020/05/26/jimmy-fallon-apologizes-over-2000-snl-blackface-skit/.

133   **"A Letter on Justice and Open Debate,":** Harper's Magazine, "A Letter on Justice and Open Debate," last modified July 7, 2020, https://harpers. org/a-letter-on-justice-and-open-debate/.

133   **"You are not being canceled":** Ross Douthat, "10 Theses About Cancel Culture," *New York Times*, last modified July 14, 2020, https://www.nytimes. com/2020/07/14/opinion/cancel-culture-.html.

134   **"Unfortunately Christians don't have":** Howard Dean (@GovHowardDean), "Unfortunately Christians don't have much a reputation for anything but . . . ," Twitter post, July 11, 2020, https://twitter.com/GovHowardDean/ status/1282013403238871040.

134   **"Goya CEO Robert Unanue":** Mike Gonzalez, "Cancel Culture Tries to Cow Goya Foods' Bob Unanue," The Daily Signal, last modified July 14, 2020, https://www.dailysignal.com/2020/07/14/ cancel-culture-tries-to-cow-goya-foods-bob-unanue/

134   **"cancel" Thomas Jefferson's candidacy:** Rick Ungar, "The Dirtiest Presidential Campaign Ever? Not Even Close!," Forbes, last modified August 20, 2012, https://www.forbes.com/sites/ rickungar/2012/08/20/the-dirtiest-presidential- campaign-ever-not-even-close/?sh=47c231833d84.

134   **editorials about President Abraham Lincoln:** "Evidence for The Unpopular Mr. Lincoln," American Battlefield Trust, https://www. battlefields.org/learn/articles/evidence-unpopular- mr-lincoln.

135   **this collective canceling:** Brooke Kato, "What is cancel culture? Everything to know about the toxic online trend," *New York Post*, last modified March 10, 2021, https://nypost.com/article/what-is-cancel-culture-breaking-down-the-toxic-online-trend/.

135   **Supreme Court rulings have protected religious liberty:** Dr. Jim Denison, "CEO faces boycott for appearing with President Trump: Explaining and responding to 'cancel culture'," Denison Forum, last modified July 16, 2020, https://www.denisonforum.org/columns/daily-article/ceo-faces-boycott-for-appearing-with-president-trump-explaining-and-responding-to-cancel-culture/.

136   **Richard Niebuhr's classic, *Christ and Culture*:** H. Richard Niebuhr, *Christ and Culture* (United States: Harper & Row, 1975).

137   **"Something is wrong when":** Francis Chan, *Crazy Love* (United States: David C. Cook, 2008).

138   **"We can really be in the world":** Henri Nouwen, "You Do Not Belong to the World," Henri Nouwen Society, https://henrinouwen.org/meditation/you-do-not-belong-to-the-world/.

140   **"Nothing would be done at all":** John Henry Newman, *Lectures on the Present Position of Catholics in England: Lecture IX* (1851).

141   **"Truth has no special time":** Albert Schweitzer, ed. Charles R. Joy, *An Anthology* (United Kingdom: Beacon Press, 1947).

7. THE PARDONABLE SIN: WHAT DOES THE BIBLE SAY ABOUT SUICIDE?

145 **According to Seacoast Church:** Bob Smietana, "Friends mourn Darrin Patrick, megachurch pastor and author, who died of apparent 'self-inflicted gunshot wound'," Religion News Service, last modified May 8, 2020, https://religionnews. com/2020/05/08/friends-mourn-darrin-patrick-megachurch-pastor-and-author-who-died-unexpectedly/.

145 **More Americans than ever before:** Dennis Thompson, "More Americans suffering from stress, anxiety and depression, study finds," CBS News, last modified April 17, 2017, https://www.cbsnews. com/news/stress-anxiety-depression-mental-illness-increases-study-finds/.

145 **Anxiety disorders are the most common:** "Understanding Disorders: What is Anxiety and Depression?," Anxiety & Depression Association of America, https://adaa.org/understanding-anxiety.

145 **direct link between anxiety and opioid use:** Nick Zagorski, "Many Prescription Opioids Go to Adults With Depression, Anxiety," Psychiatric News, last modified August 17, 2017, https://psychnews. psychiatryonline.org/doi/full/10.1176/appi. pn.2017.8a13.

146 **two to three times more likely:** "Substance Use," Anxiety & Depression Association of America, https://adaa.org/understanding-anxiety/ co-occurring-disorders/substance-abuse.

146 **Anxiety is linked to:** "Pain, anxiety, and

depression," Harvard Health Publishing: Harvard Medical School," last modified June 5, 2019, https://www.health.harvard.edu/mind-and-mood/pain-anxiety-and-depression.

146   **related anxiety directly to suicide:** Claire Mokrysz, "Patients with anxiety disorders are more likely to have suicidal thoughts and actions, says recent review," National Elf Service, The Mental Elf, last modified September 10, 2013, https://www.nationalelfservice.net/mental-health/anxiety/patients-with-anxiety-disorders-are-more-likely-to-have-suicidal-thoughts-and-actions-says-recent-review/.

146   **one in four young adults:** Brianna Ehley, "CDC: One quarter of young adults contemplated suicide during pandemic," Politico, last modified August 13, 2020, https://www.politico.com/news/2020/08/13/cdc-mental-health-pandemic-394832.

146   **eight times as likely:** Jean Twenge, "Coronavirus pandemic takes staggering toll on mental health in US," Live Science, last modified May 8, 2020, https://www.livescience.com/coronavirus-pandemic-mental-health-toll.html.

146   **"emotional distress is ubiquitous":** Betty Pfefferbaum and Carol S. North, "Mental Health and the Covid-19 Pandemic," *The New England Journal of Medicine*, last modified August 6, 2020, https://www.nejm.org/doi/full/10.1056/NEJMp2008017.

146   **isolation created by stay-at-home restrictions:** Kevin Baxter, "Isolation and

boredom of staying at home can be harmful in their own way, experts say," *Los Angeles Times*, last modified April 25, 2020, https://www.latimes. com/california/story/2020-04-25/isolation-and-boredom-of-staying-at-home-can-be-harmful-in-their-own-way-doctors-say.

147   **The scope of the issue:** Sources for this study include: *Catechism of the Catholic Church*, second edition English translation; the National Center for Injury Prevention and Control (www.ced.gov/ncipc); . T. Clemons, "Suicide," *International Standard Bible Encyclopedia*, ed. Geoffrey W. Bromiley(Grand Rapids: Eerdmans, 1988) 4:652–3; A. J. Droge, "Suicide," *The Anchor Bible Dictionary*, ed. David Noel Freedman (New York: Doubleday, 1992) 6:225–31; Milton A. Gonsalves, *Fagothey's Right and Reason: Ethics in Theory and Practice*, 9th ed. (Columbus: Merrill Publishing Company, 1989) 246–8; the Suicide Awareness Voices of Education (www.save.org); and the American Association of Suicidology (www.suicidology.org).

147   **suicide rates increased 25 percent:** Susan Scutti, "US suicide rates increased more than 25% since 1999, CDC says," CNN, last modified June 22, 2018, https://www.cnn.com/2018/06/07/health/suicide-report-cdc.

147   **suicide is the second-leading cause of death:** "Suicide by Age," Suicide Prevention Resource Center, https://www.sprc.org/scope/age.

147   **Suicide rates are much higher:** Benedict Carey, "Defying Prevention Efforts, Suicide Rates Are Climbing Across the Nation," *New York Times*,

last modified June 7, 2018, https://www.nytimes.com/2018/06/07/health/suicide-rates-kate-spade.html.

147 **Suicide rates have grown exponentially for women:** Rae Ellen Bichell, "Suicide Rates Climb In U.S., Especially Among Adolescent Girls," NPR, last modified April 22, 2016, https://www.npr.org/sections/health-shots/2016/04/22/474888854/suicide-rates-climb-in-u-s-especially-among-adolescent-girls.

147 **white, middle-aged men account for 70 percent of all suicides:** Philip Perry, "This may be responsible for the high suicide rate among white, American men," Big Think, last modified July 2, 2017, https://bigthink.com/philip-perry/this-may-be-responsible-for-the-high-suicide-rate-among-white-american-men.

147 **more than half . . . did not have a known mental health condition:** Scutti.

152 **Catechism of the Catholic Church:** *Catechism of the Catholic Church: Second Edition*, https://www.usccb.org/sites/default/files/flipbooks/catechism/.

161 **legal in nine US states:** CNN Editorial Research, "Physician-Assisted Suicide Fast Facts," CNN, last modified June 11, 2020, https://www.cnn.com/2014/11/26/us/physician-assisted-suicide-fast-facts/index.html.

161 **PAD is available to one in five Americans:** Alexander Gelfand, "TAKING A STAND ON PHYSICIAN-ASSISTED SUICIDE: Seeking a More Engaged Role to Aid Terminally Ill Patients,"

Think, Case Western Reserve University, https://
case.edu/think/spring2017/physician-assisted-
suicide.html#.YHSf4ehKjiP.

161 **"doctors should be allowed by law":** Megan
Brenan, "Americans' Strong Support for Euthanasia
Persists," Gallup, last modified May 31, 2018,
https://news.gallup.com/poll/235145/americans-
strong-support-euthanasia-persists.aspx.

161 **"Euthanasia" is derived from the Greek
words:** For further discussion of the terms and
issues involved in euthanasia, see David K. Clark
and Robert V. Rakestraw, *Readings in Christian
Ethics* (Grand Rapids: Baker, 1996) 2:95–101. Other
sources which have informed my study include
David Theo Goldberg, *Ethical Theory and Social Issues:
Historical Texts and Contemporary Readings* (New York:
Holt, Rinehart and Winston, Inc., 1988) 388–419;
and Robert D. Orr, Dvaid L. Schiedermayer, and
David B. Biebel, *Life and Death Decisions* (Colorado
Springs, Colorado: NavPress, 1990) 151–65.

163 **10,000 to 25,000 PVS patients:** Kenneth V.
Iserson, "Persistent Vegetative State," Encyclopedia
of Death and Dying, http://www.deathreference.
com/Nu-Pu/Persistent-Vegetative-State.html.

164 **the scriptural description of humanity:**
A helpful introduction to this complex subject is
Robert V. Rakestraw, "The Persistent Vegetative
State and the Withdrawal of Nutrition and
Hydration," in Clark and Rakestraw, 2:116–31.

169 **twelve "suicide warning signs":** "Injury
Prevention & Control," Centers for Disease Control
and Prevention, last modified March 9, 2021,

https://www.cdc.gov/injury/features/be-there-prevent-suicide/index.html.

170 **"The Kate Spade Conversation":** Janet Denison, "The Kate Spade Conversation," Christian Parenting, last modified June 7, 2018, http://www.christianparenting.org/articles/kate-spade-conversation/.

170 **the following indicators help buffer people:** "Suicide Prevention: Risk and Protective Factors," Centers for Disease Control and Prevention, last modified January 25, 2021, https://bit.ly/3bXdict

171 "**Mental pain is less dramatic**": C. S. Lewis, *The Problem of Pain* (United States, HarperOne, 2001), 161.

171 **"There are no *ordinary* people":** C. S. Lewis, *The Weight of Glory* (United States: Harp